IBM DataPower Handbook

Second Edition
Volume I: DataPower Intro & Setup

G000067524

Bill Hines

Ozair Sheikh

John Rasmussen

Jim Brennan

Wild Lake Press

Also Available or Coming Soon! New volumes on Networking, Development, B2B.

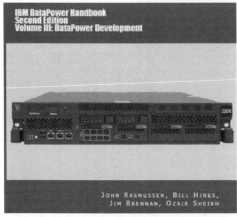

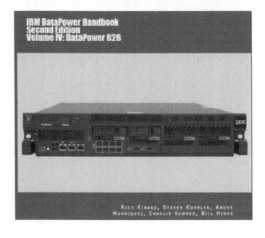

IBM DataPower Appliance Handbook
Second Edition, Volume I

The authors have taken care in the preparation of this book, but make no express or implied warranty of any kind and assume no responsibility for errors and omissions. No liability is assumed for incidental or consequential damages with or arising out of the use of the information or programs contained herein.

Note to U.S. Government Users: Documentation related to restricted right. Use,, duplication, or disclosure is subject to restrictions set forth in GSA ADP Schedule Contract with IBM Corporation.

The following terms are trademarks or registered trademarks of International Business Machines Corporation in the United States, other countries, or both: IBM, the IBM logo, IBM Press, CICS, Cloudscape, DataPower, DataPower device, DB2, developerWorks, DFS, Domino, Encina, IMS, iSeries, NetView, Rational, Redbooks, Tivoli, TivoliEnterprise, and WebSphere. Java and all Java-based trademarks and logos are trademarks or registered trademarks of Oracle and/or its affiliates. Microsoft, Windows, Windows NT, and the Windows logo are trademarks of Microsoft Corporation in the United States, other countries, or both. VMWare is a registered trademark or trademark of VMWare, Inc. in the United States and/or other jurisdictions. UNIX is a registered trademark of The Open Group in the United States and other countries. Linux is a registered trademark of Linus Torvalds in the United States, other countries, or both. Other company, product, or service names may be trademarks or service marks of others.

Version 2.0

ISBN: 0990907651

ISBN-13: 978-0990907657

LCCN: 2014918305

Wild Lake Press

Lake Hopatcong, NJ, USA

www.wildlakepress.com

Please send questions to info@wildlakepress.com and errors/corrections to errata@wildlakepress.com and include the book title and page.

To my mother Carol, who encouraged me to learn, read, and write; to my wonderful, beautiful wife Lori who inspires me and makes me laugh when I need it most; to my children Jennifer, Brittany, and Derek and step-daughters Loriana and Marie; to my sisters Donna and Patty, and the rest of my extended family, who are always there for me; and last but not least, in memory of my beloved father. —Bill Hines

To my mother Marilyn, who has shown me the strength and joy of family and the skills of perseverance; and in memory of my father James, an Officer and a Gentleman, "born on the crest of a wave and rocked in the cradle of the deep." And most of all, to my sons Alex and Nick, who provide me with continuous pride and joy. —John Rasmussen

To my beautiful wife Jennifer and wonderful children Emily, Patrick, and Madison who have all been very patient and supportive of my goals and aspirations even when it meant weekends and late nights away from them. Also to my parents, who always encouraged me to learn and persevere. —Jim Brennan

To my dear wife Khadijah, for her unconditional love and support; and my son Yunus for bringing out the best in me; to my parents who instilled good values and a strong work ethic; and my siblings for their encouragement. —Ozair Sheikh

Contents

Preface: What's New in DataPower and the Handbook

Author's Note: This book was updated in June 2015 to include updates for firmware version 7.2 as well as the new Chapter 3, "Common DataPower Use Cases."

You've come a long way, baby. That's what we'd say to a modern DataPower appliance if we could talk to it (Ok, some of us do...). In the first edition of this book, we opened with an analogy between these products and household appliances. That's still true (so, we left it in). However, placing the former Easter-egg colored appliances next to today's black, mean-looking generation would be akin to setting your grandmother's washing machine next to a modern model.

We have always compared DataPower appliances to old-school household appliances because the analogy fits—few controls, simply designed to do a few things easily *and* very well (purpose-built). Today's household appliances have changed – more blinking lights, more settings, even connecting to the Internet. And as such, our beloved DataPower appliances have also changed.

In reading the Afterword section, which is essentially intact from the first edition of this book (where it was a Foreword), there are strong hints that the appliances were originally targeted at optimizing XML and SOA use cases and flows. As the IT world has changed since 2008, so have these products. They have morphed beyond those capabilities, and now extend their benefits to use cases like sensors/Internet of Things, API Management, cloud/virtual computing, mobile, Web 2.0, and as usual, just about anything else you can throw at them.

We have updated the "DataPower Evolution" appendix, but wanted to kick off this second edition by providing a quick summary of the changes to the product line and our Handbook since we first published this book in December 2008. If you are not familiar with DataPower, you may want to skip that information, as it discusses concepts that are not explained in detail until the main sections of the book.

We have decided to self-publish this second edition, which gives us more control and allows us to get the content and any subsequent updates to our readers in a much more agile fashion.

We have also decided to publish the book in separate volumes, each consisting of related chapters. In the first edition, the book was broken into 'Parts' and these will translate to the volumes we intend to release for the second edition. This will allow us to get the book to you sooner, and as the DataPower hardware and firmware change, or as we find errors and omissions, we will update these published volumes. The up side is that you won't have to wait another six years for new content! Of course, we intend to continue to update the entire book to reflect the many changes in the DataPower world, and the current state of the product line.

This new, flexible publishing model will allow for on-demand printing of hard-copy as well as e-book availability. It will also allow our faithful readers to pick and choose which volumes apply to them. For example, developers may be interested in the volumes on development. This first volume will be lighter on technical content than the other volumes, as in the first edition. There are, however, additional appendices in this volume that we think will serve as invaluable references.

We have also moved some of the content that is typically at the front of the book to the rear of this one, as many authors are now doing, so that you have more of the actual 'good stuff' to read while using the "Look Inside" or e-book free sample tools to 'try before you buy.' One example is the Foreword, which was moved to the end as an Afterword for this very reason. As far as pricing is concerned, we don't have complete control over that, as Amazon sets it automatically, and has the right to change it. If you enjoy the book, please support us with good reviews. Please send any errors or omissions to info@wildlakepress.com.

In the first edition of this book's DataPower Evolution appendix, the hardware line from the original 9001 design through the 9004 models (which were the latest at the time) was covered. Since then, the 9005 line appeared in 2011. With it, the previous color-coding scheme went away (you can have any color you want now, as long as it's black), and two primary hardware platforms were introduced—a 1U XG45 DataPower Service Gateway and 2U XI52 Integration Appliance and XB62 B2B Appliance. As this second edition gets published, the announcement of the new 9006 hardware is hot off the presses.

Gone are our old friends the green XA35 XML accelerator model, the silver XM70 Low Latency Messaging appliance, and the yellow XS40 XML security appliance (which morphed into a new more capable model). Newly arrived are the long-awaited software or 'virtual' appliances, which we will cover in depth. Some of the other IBM appliances that were based on DataPower hardware (but not running its OS) are gone, others remain (XC10 Caching Appliance, XH40 Cast Iron Appliance), and one is new (MessageSight). Two XI50-based blade derivatives were also introduced. We will touch on, but not focus on, these related products. Our focus will be the current models in the 9005 and 9006 line, as well as their virtual implementations.

The IT world has changed dramatically since our first edition was published. New paradigms such as cloud computing, mobile, sensors/Internet of Things, APIs have risen to the forefront, and with them exciting new capabilities in DataPower's firmware. As such, these are no longer strictly "SOA" products, and the naming has been changed to reflect that—known now as "IBM DataPower Gateway Appliances" (see Chapter 1, "An Introduction to DataPower Appliance"). WebSphere Appliance Management Center (WAMC) was released as a much-improved *free* GUI tool (over the former ITCAM SE for DataPower) for managing multiple appliances. In May of 2015, IBM announced that existing WAMC capabilities and enhancements will be delivered using the open-source Appliance Management Center (AMC) project, available at https://github.com/ibm-datapower/appliance-management-center. You can learn more about WAMC at http://www-

01.ibm.com/support/docview.wss?uid=swg24032265. The Application Optimization (AO) feature was added, which has proven very popular and adds tremendous features.

We will cover all of these new capabilities and use cases to the best of our abilities. This is yet another reason for breaking the second edition into volumes—our already voluminous book may have been too much for mere mortals to wield! In addition, several new IBM software products such as IBM API Management, IBM Bluemix, and IBM MobileFirst Platform (formerly IBM Worklight) either directly incorporate or depend on DataPower, so we will address those use cases as well in this book.

The first edition of this book covered the firmware through version 3.8.2. Below is a recap of the major features added in each firmware version through V7.2, which is the latest as of this writing. You can find additional details by reading the release notes on the IBM web site.

- 4.0/4.01 (June 2011)
    - WTX auditing and logging
    - Auto-sync for WSRR
    - MQFTE & ebXML (B2B appliance)
    - Memory management & monitoring improvements
    - Tivoli Access Manager (TAM) debugging
- 4.02 (December 2012)
    - ARP takeovers
    - SLM enhancements
    - SQL return values

- - Tivoli Security Policy Manager 7.1.0.2 integration
  - Kerberos token support for AAA
- 5.0 (June 2012)
  - OAuth support
  - Tivoli Access Manager (TAM) Privilege Attribute Certificate, Extended User Attributes, TAM local mode support
  - Multi-Reference Enveloped Signature & Kerberos Service Ticket Caching
  - WS-Proxy SLA & WS-MediationPolicy Support
  - WSRR Subscription Enhancements
  - IP Multicast for SLM Peering
  - Multiple SLM Actions & Date Range Support
  - Interoperability Test Service
  - JSON Enhancements
- 6.0 (June 2013)
  - Gateway functionality for API Management V2.
  - Integration with IBM Worklight for securing/transforming mobile traffic.
  - Improved REST/JSON support and JSONiq
  - XQuery 1.0 support
  - Improved OAuth 2.0 and new support for Kerberos constrained delegation & TLS 1.1/1.2

- Embedded On-Demand Router functionality for WAS ND environments
- Response caching on-the-box & seamless integration with elastic caching XC10 appliances
- Ability to create & deploy common DataPower configuration patterns
- System z IMS transaction enhancements
- AO option available on XG45 appliance

- 6.01 (December 2013)
  - AO option available on XB62 B2B appliance
  - NIST SP800-131a & FIPS 140-2 Level 1 support
  - Globalization (G11n) support
  - Usability & serviceability enhancements

- 7.0 (June 2014)
  - Gateway Script (JavaScript-based programming model)
  - Virtual Edition for Developers
  - Citrix Xen-server support for virtual DataPower
  - 802.3ad link aggregation for network port teaming
  - SFTP on XG45
  - WebSocket proxy support

- 7.1 (October 2014)

- New product name - IBM DataPower Gateway Next generation hardware platform - 9006 hardware appliance
- Single modular product offered in both physical and virtual form factors
- ISAM proxy module
- B2B module - enables B2B virtual functionality
- Integration module
- Kerberos S4U2Self
- Common Criteria EAL4 certification for V6.0.x
- 7.2 (June 2015)
  - Amazon Elastic Compute Cloud (EC2) and SoftLayer CloudLayer Computing Instance (CCI) support for additional public cloud environment support
  - Secure Gateway Service for secure connections between IBM BlueMix cloud applications and on premise services
  - Elliptic Curve Cryptography (ECC) for TLS, Server Name Indication (SNI), and Perfect Forward Secrecy (PFC) support for protection against malicious protocol attacks
  - JSON Web Encryption (JWE), JSON Web Signature (JWS), JSON Web Key (JWK) and JSON Web Token (JWT) support for secure REST service access

- XML support using GatewayScript, JavaScript-based runtime or mediation between Systems of Engagement (e.g. client, mobile, sensors) and Systems of Record (backend systems)
- DevOps capability through a new management API based on REST
- Enhanced IMS database support
- IBM eXtremeScale 8.6+ support for distributed caching scenarios
- IBM Security Access Manager (ISAM) migration tools for easier promotion between ISAM and DataPower ISAM module
- Enhance security intelligence and compliance through integration with QRadar security information and event management (SIEM) platform
- WebSphere Transformation Extender (WTX) 8.4.1 support

That's it for our preface. Despite being a second edition revision/update, a lot of man hours went into this book you have bought for just a small amount of money. As always, we really hope you enjoy the labor of our love.

Bill Hines, Aboard the Sun and Stars, Lake Hopatcong NJ, USA August 7, 2014

Chapter 1

An Introduction to DataPower Appliances

What are Appliances, in the IT Sense?

Let's get one thing straight right from the start—these are not your mother's appliances!

Let's use that opening statement as a springboard for our discussion on exactly what computing appliances are, how they are used, and how they are similar and dissimilar to traditional household appliances. The use of the term 'appliance' to describe this class of IT products is no accident. It is meant to convey certain parallels to the term that is familiar to us. Think about it—what are the characteristics of your typical household appliances? Certain attributes should come to mind:

- Purpose-built—Appliances at home are typically for specialized uses—one for washing clothes, one for keeping food cold, and so on.
- Simple—Most appliances have few knobs and controls. They have simple designs due to the dedicated purpose for which they are designed. They are also reliable, so they don't need to be serviced or replaced often.

Get the picture? Now let's move the discussion to a realm where we, as IT professionals, are more comfortable—for many, that is not the realm of domestic chores!

There is a current trend in IT shops to use specialized appliances wherever possible. This is due to several factors, the primary ones being total cost of ownership (TCO), return on investment (ROI), performance, integration, ease of use, conformance to specifications, and security. To get started, we introduce you to IBM's DataPower Gateway Appliances, and then talk about how appliances can help in each of these areas. Of course, we go into much greater detail throughout this book.

Meet the Family!

As we mentioned in the Preface, since the first edition of this book was published, the 9005 line appeared. It consisted of the XG45 Service Gateway Appliance (an updated and more modular version of the old XS40), the XI52 Integration Appliance (a newer, more powerful version of the old XI50), and the XB62 B2B Appliance (a newer, more powerful version of the old XB60). At press time, the new 9006 appliance is being announced, in both its physical and virtual forms. Since its capabilities are a superset of the 9005 line, we will focus on it in this edition

The latest additions to the DataPower family will look and feel similar to their predecessors; but at first glance, you may feel the need for a reintroduction. We will hope to save you that embarrassing moment of asking for someone's name again when they have already introduced themselves to you!

The new DataPower product is now named the *IBM DataPower Gateway*. You will notice several things about the new name. The word DataPower remains since it holds a lot of historical and current value in the marketplace. The WebSphere branding is removed, although DataPower remains a WebSphere product, it is simply a matter of naming simplification. Hasn't Twitter taught us that fewer characters are better? The term *SOA* is replaced with *Gateway* to reflect the diverse workloads supported, and the evolution of the appliance from SOA—only to now include mobile, API, Web, B2B, and cloud architectures.

When we wrote the book originally, we were talking SOA and Web 2.0. The cool kids are now talking about cloud, mobile and API, and a few years from now, it will likely be something else!

Let's learn about the *adaptive-ness* of the new platform. Moving forward, there will only be a single physical 9006 DataPower appliance that utilizes an extensible and modular architecture to offer the functionality that is provided by the three 9005 products. It will do this through optional software modules on both the 2U high-density rack-mount physical appliance and the associated virtual form factor.

The base appliance functionality will provide the capabilities of the DataPower XG45 on a 2U physical appliance and virtual form factor. You can upgrade to the XI52 functionality by adding the Integration module. The XB62 capabilities can be added with the B2B module. These modules will be described in detail a bit later in this chapter. The value proposition is to protect your investment in the DataPower platform; you can simply enable optional modules on existing DataPower appliances at any time, protecting investment and lowering the total cost of ownership.

The two 9005 hardware formats are shown in Figure 1-1. The new 9006 hardware appliance is 2U rack height with two 10-gig ports and eight 1-gig ports, as well as 192 gig of RAM and RAID mirroring across two drives for a usable total of 1.2 TB. It is shown in Figure 1-2—notice that the only outward differences are two hard drives rather than four in the 9005 2U, the console connector port was moved over next to MGT0 and MGT1, and there is a second USB port (both are unused). An encrypted flash drive provides 16GB of high-speed memory for local storage. The primary hardware improvement from 9005 to 9006 is the additional memory and hard disc storage (9005 2U had 96 gig and 600gig, respectively). The local and disc caches are also significantly larger on the 9006 appliance, which factor into the performance improvements we will discuss shortly.

The 9005 and 9006 hardware platforms feature dedicated administration ports (one of which can use the IPMI Intelligent Platform Management Interface), improved hard drive RAID and capacity (with battery backup), more customer serviceable (fan, power supply, hard drives, network module) and field-serviceable components, configurable intrusion protection, and vastly improved performance. The hardware appliance continues to be a hardened rack-mount device in a tamper-evident case. An external LCD screen displays the current firmware. You can optionally add the Hardware

Security Module for FIPS140-2 level 3 compliant storage of encryption keys.

Figure 1-1 9005 1U and 2U DataPower hardware platforms.

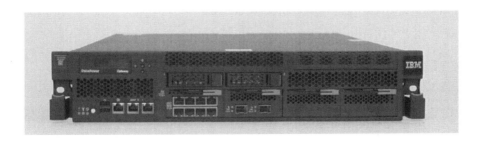

Figure 1-2 9006 2U DataPower hardware platform.

In the following sections, we discuss the feature set for the new 9006 and previous generation 9005 and their optional modules, and then move on to scenarios in which appliances can be of great value, before taking a closer look at what's under the covers.

Base IBM DataPower Gateway (9006, October 2014)

The IBM DataPower Gateway 9006 platform is a forward-thinking approach to how capabilities will be delivered in the future. The 9005 line already offered optional modules to meet requirements for additional use cases; such as Application Optimization (AO) for self-balancing and On-demand routing (ODR), Data Integration Module (DIM) option for non-XML message processing, database (ODBC), and PKCS7 features.

Firmware 7.1 and above provides a fully modular product, with additional modules to replace feature that previously were only available in specialty hardware appliances, such as the XI62 B2B model. The 9006 hardware appliance requires firmware 7.1 and higher. The following modules are available:

- Integration Module
- B2B Module
- Application Optimization Module
- TIBCO Enterprise Message Service Module
- IBM Security Access Manager (ISAM) Proxy Module

Functionally, the base appliance firmware provides the features of the XG45 appliance, including the PKCS7 capabilities that were previously part of the DIM module. The appliance provides both security and integration features and is suitable for DMZ[1] -security and trusted zone deployment scenarios.

---

[1] A DMZ is generally a front-facing "perimeter" of a network, where client traffic enters. Because it's the first point of entry into your network, and hackers have access, it must be hardened.

Integration Module

The Integration module functionally provides the core features of the XI52 appliance; namely, Any-to-Any Transformation, Database connectivity, IMS Connect, and IMS Callout. These integration capabilities are often used to connect to backend system of record infrastructure, such as IMS, mainframe systems, and databases.

The Any-to-Any Transformation functionality, as the name implies, allows you to transform non-XML (e.g. JSON, flat-file, etc...) to XML and vice versa using WebSphere Transformation Extender (WTX) maps. You can use WTX Design Studio to graphically model your input and output data types and generate WTX maps without getting into the "nuts-and-bolts" of mapping different data types. If you're more adventurous, four supported flat-file descriptor (FFD) maps give you the ability to read non-XML input and produce non-XML output from an XSL stylesheet.

The Database connectivity functionality allows you to connect with a remote database instance, such as DB2, Oracle, Sybase and Microsoft SQL Server. Quite often, you may need to interact with a database to enrich a message, or provide a service façade for your database. In a later volume, we will show how DataPower can protect against SQL injection attacks.

The IMS functionality bundles both IMS Callout and IMS Connect capabilities. DataPower appliances directly interact with IMS systems to provide accelerated access to secure data.

B2B Module

The B2B module provides unique features to support business to business (B2B) processing. This includes specialized protocol (EDIINT AS1/AS2/AS3, ebMS) and payload support (ebXML). The B2B Gateway service provides specialized support for configuring B2B interaction between partners. You can easily setup trading partner profiles for B2B governance and view partner transactions and acknowledgements using the B2B transaction viewer. The B2B module will now enable you to run B2B workloads in a virtual or cloud environment. The B2B module also contains the Any-to-Any transformation and database connectivity features that are available in the Integration module.

Application Optimization (AO) Module

The Application Optimization (AO) add-on provides network-level optimization, providing increased performance and cost savings by reducing your infrastructure footprint. The AO feature provides three key components:

1. Self-balancing: exposes a virtual IP address (VIP) to consumers to provide a highly available environment. Connections are load balanced across a set of active DataPower appliances configured within the same appliance cluster. This removes the need for a load-balancing tier in front of the appliances; especially if it was only load balancing to DataPower.

2. On Demand Routing (ODR): embedded routing technology that provides intelligent routing and load balancing to backend WebSphere Application

Server ND 8.5.5+ and WebSphere Liberty servers using the assisted lifecycle support. The ODR component within DataPower uses real-time topology, application and workload information to dynamically route backend requests.

3. Intelligent Load Distribution (ILD): intelligently load balance requests to backend servers based on server metadata from an application server. You deploy a management application on the application server. DataPower queries that application and intelligently routes requests based on the provided topology information.

This option is one of those hidden gems on the appliance, for two important reasons:

1. Increased performance: reduction of network hops on both the front (no external load balancer) and backend (route request directly to application server).

2. Cost savings: consolidate external load balancer infrastructure on the front side of DataPower and HTTP server infrastructure on the backend of DataPower.

TIBCO Enterprise Message Service (EMS) Module

TIBCO Enterprise Message Service™ (EMS) is a standards-based enterprise-messaging platform that provides asynchronous, reliable messaging between consumers and providers. DataPower can reliably poll or publish requests to a TIBCO EMS topic or queue.

IBM Security Access Manager (ISAM) Proxy Module

The IBM Security Access Manager (ISAM) proxy provides a Web SSO and access policy enforcement for Web and mobile applications. This is not the first time you have probably heard of ISAM on the appliance. The firmware already provides an ISAM client that connects to an ISAM server for authentication and authorization services. In contrast, this functionality provides reverse proxy functionality, such as session management, URL rewriting, and virtualization of backend Web applications. This component is also available within products sold by IBM's security division (ISAM for Mobile/ISAM for Web) and is now being made available on the DataPower platform. This will allow for a converged policy enforcement point on the DataPower platform that previously required deployment of separate servers for Web and SOA workloads.

In today's world, where secure data is routinely exposed beyond the walls of the enterprise, extra precautions must be taken to protect that data. Access to sensitive information can be protected based on "something you know" such as passwords, and "something you have", such as a soft token on your smartphone; and using contextual information, such as geolocation of the user. This is commonly referred to as multifactor authentication/authorization. The combined capabilities of the ISAM proxy and DataPower give you the ability to enforce a diverse set of security and integration policies for mobile applications. The ISAM proxy on DataPower provides the ability to enforce security policies deployed on ISAM for Mobile that use context-based access, one-time passwords and multi-factor (sometimes called 'step-up') authentication. Bear in mind that the ISAM for Mobile product would be needed, as well as DataPower with the ISAM Proxy Module, for these capabilities. Like DataPower, ISAM for Mobile is available in both appliance and software form factors. For those familiar with the former Tivoli Access Manager for e-Business (TAMeb) product (the predecessor to ISAM), you can think of the DataPower ISAM Proxy Module as providing the WebSEAL proxy capability that was included in that product.

By using the ISAM Proxy Module on DataPower in the DMZ, in conjunction with an ISAM server or appliance (required) in the trusted/backend zones, you can take advantage of these powerful new capabilities in a highly performant and secure manner.

DataPower Virtual Edition

The firmware and optional modules discussed in this book run on the Virtual Editions of DataPower, just as they do on the physical appliances. Using the DataPower virtual edition makes migration, testing and development all very easy and convenient.

For that reason, everything in this book, other than the physical descriptions and setup, should work on any physical or virtual appliance, as long as the proper features, firmware version, and licenses are installed. Obviously, certain features that are reliant on hardware such as the ability to add a FIPS 140-2 Level 3 HSM card, tamper-evident settings, and hardware-assisted crypto capabilities will not be available on the virtual appliances.

Virtual appliances are available in three different editions—Developer's edition, Non-Production and Production edition. The Developer's edition enables all options for free (except TIBCO EMS). The Non-Production Editions also provide all options with the exception of the TIBCO EMS and ISAM Proxy Modules. All modules must be purchased for the Production Editions. The Developer's Edition runs on VMWare Type 2 hypervisors (desktop) such as VMWare Workstation/Player/Fusion. The Production and Non-Production versions run on supported versions of VMWare ESX, ESXi, and vSphere, Citrix XenServer hypervisor, Amazon EC2, as well as IBM PureApplication™ System W1500, IBM Workload Deployer, and SoftLayer CCI, dedicated server or bare metal instance cloud platforms.

The Developer's Edition was released in April 2014, and begins with a base of firmware version v7, whereas the other two editions begin at v5. These are upgraded the same way the physical appliances are—by uploading the signed, encrypted firmware image and doing a quick reboot. The Developer Editions are licensed to a single user (for example, to run on a single developer workstation) and licensed for use in development and test environments, but the Non-Production versions can be used to create shared, multi-user development, testing and staging environments.

DataPower Cloud Editions

Cloud platforms are extremely important in today's IT landscape and architectures. DataPower's initial support was limited to IBM SoftLayer bare-metal instances in version 7.1, but with 7.2 expanded to SoftLayer CloudLayer Computing

Instance (CCI) and Amazon Elastic Compute Cloud (EC2). These cloud environments provide elastic on-demand capabilities so that workloads can be scaled at lower costs when circumstances demand more or less computing power. They are Infrastructure as a Service (IaaS) offerings. DataPower is also part of IBM's Bluemix Platform as a Service platform offering.

DataPower also provides a Secure Gateway service that can be used to securely connect IBM Bluemix applications to on premise applications in hybrid cloud architectures. This allows for quick connectivity without having to make firewall changes while still allowing controlled access. This is accomplished by using known ports (443/80) with the WebSockets protocol, to create an initial connection, initiated from DataPower instead of Bluemix. The communication is two-way since it's based on WebSockets. It also provides for load balancing and fault tolerance in these scenarios.

In the following sections, we discuss the feature set for the 9005 hardware line.

WebSphere DataPower Service Gateway XG45 (Type 7198, October 2011)

When the 9005 line was designed, the thinking was that the lower-end offering should be more modular, and be able to grow as customers encounter additional use cases. The DataPower XG45 is positioned as a security gateway, but options can be added to allow it to do much more than just security. It can in fact approach the capabilities of the XI52. However, due to the differences in memory, disk, and network capacity, it cannot match the XI52 in terms of absolute performance.

The XG45 in base form is an XML (and now JSON)-centric appliance. However, there is an available Data Integration Module (DIM) option that can be purchased before or after the sale to add non-XML message processing capability. The original XS40 was HTTP(s) only, but the XG45 includes FTP(s), JMS, MQ and MQ FTE out of the box (and later, with firmware version 7.0, SFTP). The DIM option also adds database (ODBC) and PKCS7 features.

WebSphere DataPower Integration Appliance XI52 (Type 7199, June 2011)

The DataPower XI52 is the integration appliance, as represented by the "I" in XI. Due to its integration capabilities, it is often found in the backend private network, functioning in that capacity, but it is just as suitable for the DMZ. It is built on the 2U physical format described earlier, and is a performance beast with a tremendous amount of network and internal processing capability. The database (ODBC) option can be added as an additional add-on to the appliance at the time of purchase or at a later time.

WebSphere DataPower B2B Appliance XB62 (Type 7199, June 2011)

The DataPower XB62 is also a 2U-format appliance, and is quite similar to the XI52 in many ways, but has unique features to support business to business (B2B) processing. This includes special protocols (EDIINT AS1/ AS2/AS3, ebMS, SMTP), configurations/services (B2B Gateway), and payload support (ebXML). It is the only primary DataPower appliance designed to be stateful, and it contains the ODBC database features by default, and with firmware 6.01 and after, can use the optional Application Optimization feature.

WebSphere DataPower Service Gateway XG45 & XI52 Virtual Edition (November 2012/April 2014)

As stated earlier, the virtual editions of the XG45 and XI52 run the same firmware as the physical appliances, which make migration, testing and development all very easy and convenient.

Add-on Options for XG45/XI52

As mentioned earlier, firmware 7.1 and up deliver capabilities that were previously unique to individual appliances, as modules on the 9006 platform. For those of you with 9005 appliances, the good news is that you can obtain the B2B module on your XG45 and XI52 appliances to support B2B use cases. The entire 9005 hardware line (XG45/XI52/XB62) supports the ISAM proxy add-on for reverse proxy and authentication scenarios.

Typical Usages of Appliances

While the appliances are quite versatile and can thus be used to solve many different types of problems (and implementers have been quite creative in this regard), we find there are a few common use cases that are typical. These generally focus around *security*, *integration*, *control*, and *optimization* and are delivered in a policy-driven fashion, applicable to Web, mobile, API, SOA, B2B and cloud workloads. We will cover some of these use cases at a high level in this section, however please refer to Chapter 3, "Common DataPower Use Cases" for a more detailed and expanded discussion of deployment scenarios and usages.

The DataPower platform is a purpose-built solution providing a lower total cost of ownership comparatively to building a similar solution in-house or using existing "off-the-shelf" products. In the following sections, we discuss each of these in more detail. We will also elaborate on common topologies and deployment patterns in Chapter 3, "Common DataPower Use Cases."

Security

Let's think about what it would take to deploy a software-based proxy product in the DMZ. Each of the layers of the 'typical server' shown in Figure 1-3 require specialized skills to install and maintain. Particularly for DMZ deployments, the server hardware itself must be hardened (DataPower is hardened out of the box!) In highly secure environments, this can involve removing or disabling any components that might allow information to be taken from the server, such as USB ports and writable CD/DVD drives. The operating system must also be hardened, removing unneeded components such as telnet and sendmail[2]. Often, these changes result in other layers of the software stack not installing or operating properly. If you are successful in installing the application software stack, it must be hardened as well. These are common requirements for high

---

[2] The Center for Internet Security (http://cisecurity.org/) has papers showing how to harden various platforms, as well as scoring tools to see how well your platform is hardened.

security environments such as financial companies, intelligence services, and military applications.

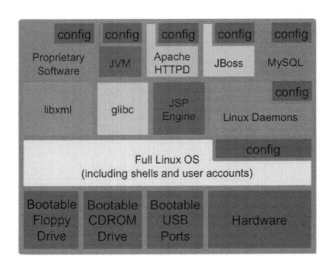

Figure 1-3 Typical server stack components.

Although software-based DMZ components can be hardened successfully, it is a lot of work, it is complex (the enemy of security), and there is a high degree of likelihood that somewhere along the line, a mistake was made that will be found by those wishing to compromise the system. Compare this with the simplicity of installing a dedicated, highly secure hardware appliance, purpose built to do a few things well with fairly simple administrative interfaces, as shown in Figure 1-4.

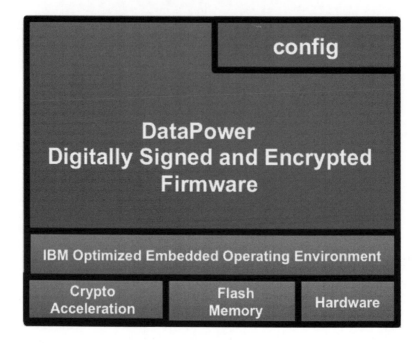

Figure 1-4 DataPower appliance components.

The appliances are hardened out of the box. For example:

- They are designed with security in mind from the ground up, before anything else.
- They are shipped secure by default; virtually every feature is disabled, including the network adapters and administrative interfaces (except for the console connector used to do initial bootstrap). If you want something, you must turn it on!
- They have an encrypted file system.
- They have no exposed Java, print services, or shareable file system.

- They are tamper-evident—backing out the screws on the case can disable the appliance or trip log alerts (configurable).
- They have specialized secure handling of cryptographic keys and certificates.
- They have an embedded operating system, not prone to the known exposures of common operating systems.
- They reject messages by default, unless specifically accepted by configured policies.

The age-old rule for the DMZ is to terminate client connections there and then proxy the message over secure connections to the backend from trusted DMZ servers. However, in the field we find even more stringent security policies that do not warrant *any* traffic (even proxied through these secure intermediaries) to the backend until the client is authenticated and authorized, policies are enforced, and messages are validated to be schema-correct and contain no threats. This is referred to as perimeter security and is an increasingly common requirement, driving sales of DMZ security products. Later, we will show how DataPower appliances can also solve this problem.

Another requirement for DMZ components is to virtualize or hide the implementation details of backend servers and applications. Typical DMZ products interact only with the protocol layer of the network stack, so they can hide things like hostname/IP, ports, and URIs, whereas message-centric application proxies such as DataPower appliances can virtualize on a much more intelligent basis and can analyze the entire message stream for security and routing purposes.

A strong reason for using these types of appliances is the burgeoning risk of systems becoming compromised by message-based threats. Just as once upon a time we felt HTTP to be innocuous, today we are susceptible to underestimating what can be done by virtue of message content. In the "Message Threats" chapter in a later volume, we show how entire infrastructures can be brought down using small, simple, well-formed message files.

Another common security problem is a mismatch in the specification levels or credential formats of various technologies across large corporate IT infrastructures. For example, consider a marketing IT silo running on Microsoft®.NET using WS-Security 1.0 and SPNEGO credentials for identity, and a manufacturing silo using IBM WebSphere Application Server (WAS), WS-Security 1.1, and LTPA credentials for identity. In today's complex architectures, a single transaction may have to pass through both environments, which presents challenges. Because DataPower appliances implement a wide range of the latest specifications and credential formats, they can be used to transform messages and credentials to fit the requirements of each step of the way. Notice that this can be used to achieve cross-platform single-sign on (SSO), to avoid repeatedly asking the users to log in.

Control

DataPower appliances are often deployed at the edge of your network. They are the entry point for your transactions (and are often the first to be blamed, *incorrectly*, when errors occur!). As requests flow downstream into backend systems, each server may provide different qualities of service or support a certain transaction threshold. The DataPower appliances can process high-volumes of transactions, so they are unlikely to become a performance bottleneck in your infrastructure. Furthermore, you can deploy Service Level Management (SLM) policies at a granular level to manage traffic flowing through DataPower to backend servers. This allows you to enforce service level agreements (SLA) between consumers and providers and provide stability to backend systems by preventing them from receiving unsupportable volumes of messages.

You can use WebSphere Service Registry and Repository (WSRR) to author and govern SLA policies based on WS-Mediation policy, which can be deployed in a non-disruptive fashion. This will allow you to support continuous delivery, and easily operate within a DevOps environment.

Optimization

XML is the foundation on which many modern architectures are built—it has evolved into SOAP for Web services and is found across the breadth and depth of the SOA stack and related specifications. Over time, it has evolved from a simple markup language to something quite complex and sophisticated. Of course, the problem as far as performance is concerned is that XML is fairly easy for humans to read, but not for computers. It is a verbose representation of data and typically requires significant resources in terms of CPU power and memory to process. This overhead is typically found in parsing the XML document into an in-memory representation and in validating the XML against its schema file.[3]

While XML has matured and is rather old-school, today we have increased use of JSON, which is where XML was some time ago in terms of things like security, schema, and threat detection. JSON is a first-class citizen on DataPower, and the tools can be found there to safely process or mediate JSON messages to your back end systems. Handling XML and JSON crypto and validation tasks on a high-performance platform like DataPower means freeing up more cycles on your back-end systems, since they no longer have to perform those intensive tasks or spend cycles in exception handling logic—not to mention better up-time and reliability by avoiding crashes caused by bad messages.

Consider the impact of parsing and validating the storm of JSON/XML/SOAP (or other) documents that hit your systems during peak production levels. Now consider the overhead of security that may be required for those messages—validating client identities against LDAP servers, verifying digital signatures, and decrypting encrypted data. This requires a tremendous amount of processing power and time and robs precious cycles away from what your backend systems should really be doing—focusing on transactional business logic!

Also consider the absolute waste of expending these cycles for messages that come in badly formed, with schema violations or security issues. The cycles expended on

---

[3] An XML schema definition file (XSD) is a set of rules for how the file should look and what it should contain, including optional and required elements.

processing them and handling errors are wasted. Figure 1-5 shows a graph demonstrating the CPU overhead of various common tasks. (Notice the parsing level is low here—the main hit when parsing is memory utilization, not CPU usage.) Notice the impact of security operations. This can be helped somewhat with hardware-assisted acceleration on standard servers, but this involves yet another procurement and administrative cost. Also note that intentionally abusing these security features to consume CPU resources is one way of mounting attacks.

A grand solution for this, of course, is to use appliances to do all that heavy lifting at near wire speed. As you will see when we discuss the appliance characteristics, they are amazingly fast and can handle these tasks at orders of magnitude faster than software-based solutions running on standard servers. Now focus on another scenario—one where the appliance makes sure that only clean traffic gets to the backend systems. Imagine the huge differential in available processing power on the backend if the validation and security tasks are done by the time the traffic gets there. The appliances can validate schemas, verify signatures, decrypt the data, and more. This can often result in huge performance returns, depending on considerations such as message sizes, cipher strengths, network latency, and so forth.

Speaking of message sizes, this is often another major stumbling block for Java-based software systems. In modern day real-world systems, we are now seeing huge messages on the order of hundreds of megabytes or even gigabytes in size. The conundrum is how to process these, given constraints on maximum JVM heap sizes in many server platforms. Due to aggressive built-in streaming and compression, appliances can handle messages larger than their actual memory space.

Figure 1-5 CPU performance impact of common tasks.

On another message-related topic, consider applications that do transformation between differing schemas; for example, an application that consumes purchase orders and must understand a variety of incoming purchase order formats from business partners, and then transforms each into the one "golden" purchase order schema that this company uses. These transformations can be quite expensive to process (see Figure 1-5) and result in bloated application code. We all know that line-for-line, application code is expensive in terms of programmer time, testing, and debugging.

Now consider the effect on the application if the transformations were moved out to the appliance on the frontend so that the backend application now gets only the one "golden" schema format. Yes, our application has gone on quite a diet, is less expensive to maintain, and is much faster. One field scenario consisted of a frontend cluster of Java EE applications to do such transformations to keep the cluster of business logic applications behind it lightweight. However, since this was running on a platform that charged for CPU time, and given the overhead of message transformations shown in Figure 1-5, it was expensive. The solution was to move the transformation layer out to DataPower appliances. The result was a huge cost saving and much faster processing.

Integration

In the previous section, we discussed a scenario in which the appliance could be used to bridge differences in standards specifications (WS-Security v1.0 versus v1.1) and identity credentials (SPNEGO versus LTPA) across systems. This is one good example of easily integrating disparate platforms, particularly when the standards and specifications are in flux. It is difficult for software-based solutions running on standard servers and products to keep up with this, often needing complex updates to multiple components. On the appliance, you simply load a firmware update to get the latest and greatest.

NOTE—Firmware Versions Used for This Book

The recommendations, advice, and practices shown in this book are generally applicable to firmware versions through 7.2 and based on the DataPower Gateway (9006). However, much of the information in this book is "timeless" in that it represents information that is generally accepted as "best practices" in our experience for most situations, and unrelated to specific firmware versions.

However, there are other issues that arise when integrating different platforms. Consider a scenario in which a medium-sized business XYZ Corp has its infrastructure running on legacy platforms and technologies, perhaps mainframe-based EDI. The business partners that they depend on have long since moved their platforms to Web 2.0 and are telling poor XYZ Corp that they can no longer afford to support XYZ's legacy interface to that system, and they must provide a modern, Web 2.0/mobile/API-friendly REST/JSON interface or lose the business. This puts XYZ in a bad position; what will it cost to retrain its programmers, rewrite its COBOL applications, and revamp the backend infrastructure? Likely, it would be a staggering amount!

A common solution to this problem is to place appliances at the front of the network as proxies, configure a few proxies to mediate and transform the messages, credentials, and protocols, begin receiving the new messages from the now-happy business partners, and convert them on-the-fly to EBCDIC EDI or COBOL Copybook messages and send them over MQ or IMS Connect to the legacy backend. The backend does not have to change, and no programs have to be rewritten—a win-win! In the past, we have used Web services as the 'modern' front end, but with mobile devices becoming a popular channel, the use of REST/JSON is rising. You have probably heard the terms 'System of Engagement' and 'System of Record'. The former term is used to describe user engaged systems (mobile technologies, email, collaboration systems) that enable quick access to key information, often displayed on smaller device form factors (smartphones, tablets, etc). This is where REST/JSON is being used due its light weight and simplicity. The latter term describes the process of integrating with backend SOA, mainframe/legacy, and database systems. This is where SOAP and Web services are still the enterprise standard due their maturity and interoperability with many systems. DataPower supports Web 2.0 REST/JSON to Web Services/SOAP, providing similar benefits. The DataPower appliances can handle any message transformation scenario, meaning that messages can be transformed to the appropriate format for any intended backend.

Due to the variety of protocols (HTTP, FTP, MQ, JMS/JFAP, IMS, NFS, TIBCO, MQ, ODBC, and so on) supported by the DataPower appliances, there is a wealth of opportunity for protocol bridging, content enrichment, and integration between platforms. Notice that the previous scenario involved message transformation, but protocol mediation is often just as important.

Another common and age-old scenario related to integrating platforms is dynamic, content-based routing. Because it is often a requirement to make dynamic routing decisions "on the edge of the network," we have DMZ Web servers, proxies, and load balancers to handle this. The problem is that they can understand only the protocol and not the payload of the message. To accomplish the goal, applications place some value in the protocol header to facilitate content-based routing.

As an example, in the past if we wanted any purchase orders over one million dollars to be routed to high-priority servers, the sending application would place a cookie or attribute in an HTTP header or URL parameter. The Web server, proxy, or load balancer in the DMZ would be configured to check for this and then route the traffic accordingly. The problem with this scenario is that you have to put this hack in the applications and the HTTP payload, potentially disclose message data to attackers, and involve the sender/client. This solution doesn't scale, because if you continually do this, the HTTP header and application code become more bloated. Plus, you may inadvertently put sensitive data into those headers, which could then be discovered and used by those wishing to compromise your system – even if you are using message level security to protect your data and think you are secure!

Because gateway appliances are multi-lingual in terms of many message formats they understand, and can use technologies such as JSONiq, XPath, and XQuery, they can check inside the message payload to look for the actual purchase order value rather than alter the application and HTTP header. If the message is encrypted, you don't need to expose this by externalizing the data; you can just decrypt the message and check the value, and then route accordingly. The client in this case does not have to be complicit—the routing is truly dynamic and transparent.

One last important feature in regard to the integration story is the use of appliances as an Enterprise Service Bus (ESB). The appliances fulfill the general requirements of an ESB by virtue of their strong routing, transformation, mediation, and protocol-switching capabilities. However, IBM has a dedicated ESB product—IBM Integration Bus (IIB). Although DataPower may be used as a highly secure and performant ESB gateway or on-ramp, IIB has additional features such as transactionality, persistent message handling, and the capability to work in other programming languages. We discuss this in Chapter 3, "Common DataPower Deployment Patterns" in this book, and the "Multi-Protocol Gateway" chapter in a later volume.

To Lower Total Cost of Ownership (TCO)

Refer back to the scenario in Figure 1-3, where there are numerous skills required to install and maintain a typical server and software stack. Now think of this in terms of the staff required and cost to the organization. With self-contained appliances, where the operating system and file system characteristics are irrelevant from an administrative perspective, this becomes much less work. The function of the appliances is dedicated and streamlined, hence the administrative tasks and interfaces tend to be as well. For example, in the scenario in Figure 1-3, you have to continually install fixes and updates at every layer of the stack. However, for appliances, you typically do this by uploading a firmware update and rebooting, which takes only minutes. In the server scenario, you have multiple different administrative consoles to manage the layers of the stack; with the appliances, you have only one console.

The TCO return does not solely manifest itself in the setup and administration of the platform. Consider the silo example in the prior section—where various areas of a corporate IT infrastructure are running Web services across different platforms, such as those from IBM, Microsoft, and BEA. If the corporation has one set of policies for security and service level monitoring (SLM) that need to be implemented across all these platforms, then it must be done multiple times, by multiple people who each possess skills on a particular platform. Not only is the configuration redundant and therefore expensive, but this problem is repeated each time it needs to change, and there is always the risk that the policy will not be implemented exactly the same on each platform, which can lead to security holes or application failures. This is depicted in Figure 1-6.

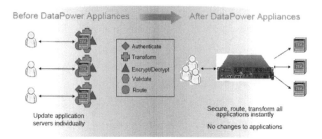

Figure 1-6 Redundant administration versus simplified appliance model.

A stronger solution can be implemented by creating a single service that acts as a Web service proxy on the DataPower appliance, importing the WSDL files for the Web services providers on each of those backend platforms, and then applying the security and SLM policies on the proxy, thereby gaining policy definition and enforcement one time for all platforms. All this is based on standards that we discuss later, not only Web services itself, but also the accompanying standards such as WS-Security for security, WS-Policy for policy definition, WS-Addressing for endpoint resolution, and WS-Management and WSDM[4] for management.

---

[4] WSDM (Web Services Distributed Management) is a Web service

A Closer Look at the DataPower Products

Now that you have a general idea what "Gateway Appliances" are, and have some familiarity with the IBM offerings in this space and what they are used for, we will describe them in more detail.

Physical Characteristics of Appliances

As stated earlier, and demonstrated in Figure 1-1, the appliances are "pizza-box," rack-mountable 2U or 1U hardware devices. The only external interfaces are a power button, status LEDs and display panel, an RJ45 console connector port, a USB port (disabled), two RJ45 Ethernet management ports, and 1-gig and 10-gig RJ45 Ethernet ports on the front, and fans and power supplies on the back. These interfaces are described in more detail in Chapter 2, "DataPower Quick Tour and Setup."

NOTE—Tamper-Evidence

On previous generations of appliances, if you were to back out the screws on the case, the tamper-protection system would engage and the appliance would 'brick' itself and have to be sent back to IBM for reset. The 9005/9006 models now allow administrative configuration of this setting, which allows for easier field servicing of internal components.

---

standard for managing and monitoring the status of Web services.

Software Architecture of Appliances

As Figure 1-4 illustrates, the DataPower firmware architecture is simple from a user perspective. There is a customized, hardened, native-code operating system kernel that implements the appliance's core functionality. The OS resides in firmware that can be updated by applying signed and encrypted firmware update files.

On top of this is a layer of functionality that is implemented in XSLT stylesheets, which are read-only and used by the system to implement certain functionality. We get into more detail in Chapter 2, "DataPower Quick Tour and Setup."

The next layer up the software stack consists of configurations developed by the user; these are the application proxies and processing policies to process message traffic for your applications.

Configuration files and application artifacts can reside in the directory structure on the file system or they can be hosted on remote servers and retrieved and cached at start-up time so that they do not ever reside on the appliance file system in the DMZ (a requirement in some highly secure environments).

Although the operating system itself and many of the appliances' implementation details are custom and purpose-built, outwardly, the appliances support many standards. A few important ones are listed here.

- JSON—JavaScript Object Notation is an open standard format that is more human-readable and lightweight than XML, and hence more useful for lightweight Web 2.0/REST flows for mobile and service traffic.

- XML—A general purpose specification for creating other markup languages—and many are built upon it, such as MathML (a markup language to describe mathematics). It is a combination of data and metadata, consisting of tagged elements to not only show the data but to describe and delineate it; for example, <po_number>12345</po_number>.

- XSD—A set of rules that an XML file must conform to. So if you want to define a purchase order XML file to use with your applications, you can create an XSD file to define the structure of that XML, which can be used to validate those incoming purchase order XML files to ensure they have the proper structures.

- SOAP—A message format used by Web services for sending and receiving XML—based messages. It is more sophisticated than "normal" XML in that its construct provides for a message header and body, among other things.

- WSDL—A language for describing Web services. It defines the services, ports, bindings, and operations that constitute the Web service, along with the endpoint information (hosts, ports, URIs) and perhaps other metadata such as policy information.

- XPath—XPath for XML is somewhat analogous in function (but not syntax) to SQL for databases. XPath allows for searching and retrieving information (nodesets) from XML documents based on some criteria.

- XQuery—A specification related to XPath that is much closer to true SQL compatibility.

- XSLT—An XML language for transforming XML documents from one format to another. If you want to transform a vendor's XML purchase order format to your own company's XML format, you can write a set of instructions in XSLT to do so.

- EXSLT—A community extension to XSLT to provide a library for things like string manipulation, date/time functions, and other miscellaneous library functions.

- JSONiq—Adds support for JSON messages in XQuery scripts.

Administrative Model

As part of the "secure by default" DataPower mantra, all remote administrative interfaces are disabled by default. The only way to enable them at appliance initialization is by bootstrapping the appliance via the console connector port or by using serial over LAN on the MGT0 port. Later, other administrative interfaces can be enabled or disabled by any configured administrative interface. We show how to do this on initialization in Chapter 2.

After you do this, you have several options for administrative interfaces. These are described in detail in the "Device Administration" and "Alternate Management

Interfaces," chapters in a later volume, but here is a brief overview:

- Command-shell Admin—This can be accessed using telnet, secure-shell (SSH), the management ports, or the console connector. The Command Line Interface (CLI) is an interface that will be familiar to many network administrators. In the most ultra-secure environments, all remote administrative interfaces are disabled, forcing all administration to be done only by those with physical access to the appliances in the datacenter, or by serial over LAN. For security purposes, telnet normally remains disabled.

- XML Management Interface—The XML Management interface provides a way to administer the appliance and obtain status information via XML-based SOAP requests. There are several different specifications that can be used, including DataPower's own SOAP Configuration Management, WS-Management, and WSDM. This interface is commonly used for automated, programmatic, or custom approaches to administration. This has past been referred to as SOMA, which is shorthand for SOAP Management.

- REST-based Management API—A lighter-weight alternative that is conducive to modern DevOps approaches to build/deploy, migration scripts, and other automated operations. This approach enables continuous delivery of new configurations through the systems lifecycle environments in development, test, and production. It is easy to integrate with build tools such as IBM UrbanCode Deploy.

- WebGUI Admin Console—This is a standard browser-based administrative interface. It is the most commonly used way to administer the appliances. However, in some high security or production environments, browser-based administration is not permitted and is allowed only in development environments.

The WebGUI is not only used for administering the appliance, it is also used to create the application proxies that are the *raison d'être* for the product. You can use the drag-and-drop capabilities of the Processing Policy editor to create work-flow type rules for requests and responses, to carry out various actions as traffic flows through the device.

Figure 1-7 shows the simplicity of dragging an Encrypt Action from the upper palette row of actions to the processing rule to encrypt a message as it passes through to its destination. From here, only the certificate to be used for the encryption needs to be configured, although there are many other advanced options that can be chosen, such as the encryption algorithm to use. Compare the ease of this to creating policies to encrypt a message on other platforms (and then factor in the performance difference). Notice in this figure that the other types of actions can be just as easily applied for tasks such as message filtering, creating or validation digital signatures, transforming messages, dynamic routing, and AAA. The Advanced Action contains a great deal more.

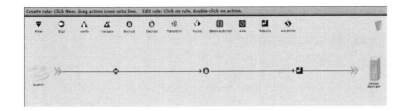

Figure 1-7 Drag and drop policy editor.

Often, the browser-based console is used only in development environments for easily building proxies, and from there, automated, scripted processes are used to deploy these configurations to test, QA and production environments, leveraging either the command-line, or SOAP-based administrative interfaces. These techniques are described in the "Build and Deploy Techniques" chapter in a later volume.

Programming Model

As shown in the previous section, most of the work in configuring the appliances is done using the friendly drag-and-drop paradigm of the Processing Policy editor. For any customized scenarios not covered by the GUI, it can be extended with custom programming.

Custom programming language options include GatewayScript (JavaScript) and XSLT, which is a full Turing-complete programming language.

XPath is an important technology for these products. Aside from custom programming done in GatewayScript or XSLT, XPath expressions are used frequently in building configurations using the WebGUI. For example, if you are building a policy to sign and/or encrypt selected nodesets in an

XML or SOAP document, you simply provide DataPower an XPath expression so that it can locate those nodesets. For non-programmer types, the DataPower WebGUI provides an easy-to-use XPath tool that enables you to load a sample document and click on the element or nodeset, and the XPath statement is generated for you.

The DataPower appliances offer much more than what standard XSLT and EXSLT have in their libraries. The appliances support crypto operations and many different protocols that are outside the domain of XSLT and EXSLT. To provide for custom programming that leverages the full scope of functionality on the appliances, they include a library of extension functions and elements that can be used for custom programming. These are covered in the chapters in Volume III, "DataPower Development."

Of course, all the power of JSON, XML, SOAP, and many of the related specifications/standards are available on the appliance. Some of the key specifications are

- WS-Security—A specification to enable message integrity, message privacy, and non-repudiation, typically using digital signatures and encryption.
- WS-Addressing—A specification to enable Web services to communicate endpoint and addressing information between themselves.
- WS-Policy—A specification that allows Web services to advertise and enforce policies for things like security and quality of service.
- JSONiq – A specification that allows query and processing of JSON data.

- OAuth – A specification that allows client applications access to external resources from a resource owner without the sharing of credentials.

DataPower as a Member of the Network Infrastructure

At their physical core and in outward appearance, the DataPower appliances are network devices. In Figure 1-1, the most apparent feature is the set of network interface jacks on the front of the appliance. They can be split up any way you choose; for example, some can be configured so that they receive client traffic and others connected to the backend private network, thereby segregating the network flows for better security and isolation.

There are also a number of network protocols supported on the appliances. These include HTTP, HTTPS, FTP, FTPS, SFTP, NFS, MQ, MQ/SSL, JMS, and Tibco EMS for application traffic, and SNMP, SMTP, sFTP, and others for administrative usage.

We've mentioned SNMP a few times, which is ubiquitous and useful for infrastructure monitoring. The appliance comes with SNMP MIB files that can be imported into your monitoring tools to set up monitoring policies, and the appliances can send out SNMP traps when critical events occur. Monitoring can also be achieved by using SOAP, as is the case with the integration with Tivoli ITCAM. There are also objects built that are useful for monitoring and auditing, such as message count and duration monitors and sophisticated service-level management tools. Most logging is done off-device, utilizing protocols such as syslog and syslog-tcp, or by writing logs to a remote NFS mount. (DataPower never shares its own file system, but can connect to shared file systems on other servers.) There is a full suite of logging formats and protocols for your use, as well as a model for specifying event notifications on various levels of granularity.

Also available is a utility for managing multiple devices, called WebSphere Appliance Management Center (WAMC). This takes the place of the former ITCAM SE for DataPower, and is vastly improved over that offering, as well as being free of charge! This utility is installed on a server or workstation and enables appliances to be grouped into managed sets in order to keep their firmware levels and configurations in sync. This can be used to configure a group of application proxies for high availability and better levels of service. It also backs up the configurations when it detects changes and allows for appliance monitoring. In May of 2015, IBM announced that existing WAMC capabilities and enhancements will be delivered using the open-source Appliance Management Center (AMC) project, available at https://github.com/ibm-datapower/appliance-management-center. It is covered in a later volume's chapter, "Multiple Device Management Tools" and can be downloaded at http://www-01.ibm.com/support/docview.wss?uid=swg24032265

We elaborate on common network topologies and deployment scenarios in Chapter 3, "Common DataPower Deployment Patterns."

Performance

DataPower can enhance the performance of any environment it is used in by offloading intensive operations such as schema validation, crypto operations, threat checking, authorization/authentication, SSL/TLS termination, and message/protocol/credential transformation from overwhelmed backend servers, freeing them up to focus on performing business logic on clean messages. However, the most common questions around DataPower center on performance of the products themselves. "Just how fast are they?" "How much faster is an XI52 than a XG45?" "How fast are the virtual editions?"

As with any question about performance, the answer is a firm "it depends." You would expect that we could give solid concrete numbers around the performance of the physical appliances, which are self-contained and easily measurable. If you hook up some large number of high-speed clients, pumping in requests to the multitude of interfaces, with back-ends stubbed out or using loopback back-ends, and not doing any real work on the transaction (such as crypto operations, transformation, etc.) you will get some astounding results. But these are the kind of unrealistic tests and results used in sales wars (typically by competitors!) and not pertinent in the real world.

As blazingly fast as the appliances are, they are typically at the mercy of other infrastructure components with which they must interact. These can include LDAP, OSCP, anti-virus, security policy, and database servers used for side calls, and of course the backend servers that DataPower passes transactions to and from. Despite DataPower's speed, if those servers are slow to respond, the bubble in the hose (DataPower) continues to grow as it queues up pending transactions. So, the only 'real' answer to the performance question is to test in *your* environment, using *your* network speeds and reliability, and *your* network component latencies, for *your* DataPower use cases. Anything else is pretty irrelevant, and would have to be delivered with a heavy dose of YMMV (your mileage may vary). The virtual appliances cloud the picture even more—the answers are heavily reliant on the platforms on which you are running them and the configuration choices that you have made, such as those related to resource allocation.

That said, there are some general rules of thumb and consistency based on results of IBM internal testing and that of a few customers who have reported performance test results (and YMMV!). In general, for typical, non-trivial use cases, and factoring out outside factors such as external server latencies and network speeds, the 9005 appliances tend to be a conservative 1.5-3x (150-300%) faster than their 9004 predecessors (using only 1 gigabit Ethernet, to be fair!), whereas 9006 appliances tend to be 3.5-6x (350 - 600%) faster than 9004.

The appliances have been shown to scale very gracefully under load, much more so than standard server software stacks. Maximum throughput is typically maintained even as user load increases beyond capacity. This is a very big deal— typical servers will plateau as the load reaches their capacity, and then begin to become unreliable and eventually crash, which is the whole point of denial of service attacks. When

DataPower appliances reach their maximum throughput (something highly unlikely in normal scenarios), they just hold steady. Use cases that process first-class message formats like XML, SOAP, and JSON perform better than those using WTX to process binary message formats, as you might expect.

Tests were run on the virtual XI52[5] appliances using 4CPU 8GB RAM, 8CPU 8GB RAM, 16CPU 96GB RAM, and 24CPU 96GB RAM configurations with CPU affinity set (except in the 24 CPU case) and client drivers set for 100 concurrent connections. Payloads were 2-5K SOAP messages over two-way SSL/TLS and non-trivial processing policies that involved AAA, digital signature validation, schema validation, message filtering (injection scan), dynamic routing, and encryption, over 10gig Ethernet. The results are shown in Figure 1-8, and again, your mileage may (and will) vary!

---

[5] An IBM X series M3 with 2 * Intel(R) Xeon(R) CPU X5670 @ 2.93GHz and 96 GB RAM. The Intel Xeon X5670 provides 2 physical CPU sockets with 6 physical cores per socket. Hyper-threading is also included, yielding 12 total threads for each CPU socket. There are 2 CPU sockets in the IBM X series M3, yielding 24 total hardware threads.

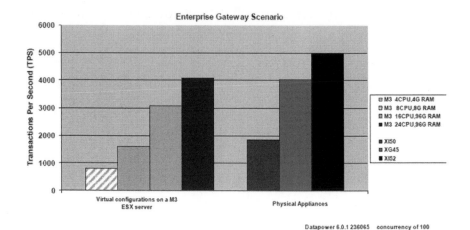

Figure 1-8 Performance results for physical versus virtual appliances.

One interesting finding is that the performance of the DataPower Virtual Edition at 24vCPUs may not scale as expected, depending on the scenario. This is due to VMWare system overhead. In this particular setup, because the physical CPUs on the server only had 12 physical cores, a server with 24 physical cores and appropriate hypervisor setting would have shown much better numbers. As throughput increases, this overhead can limit the ability to fully utilize the appliance's allocated CPUs. Scalability is very good at four through sixteen vCPUs.

For the tested scenario, the virtual edition produces a maximum of just over 4,000 TPS, which is about 80% of what the physical XI52 can do, and approximately equivalent to the physical XG45's performance. In general, a physical XI52 provides a 20% performance advantage over a physical XG45. In a JSON scenario, results were somewhat similar in terms of the physical to virtual performance.

If you wish to explore performance or these results in more detail, contact your IBM client representative to have some technical folks come in and discuss these results in detail, or proof out similar tests in your environment, and then your mileage will be more precise. IBM has data on additional tests involving binary messages, database scenarios, and SSL termination.

Summary

This chapter served as an introduction and overview of the IBM DataPower Gateway Appliances. We introduced you to the product family and ran through some use cases where the strengths of this platform are emphasized, and then took a closer look and discussed at a glance how the appliances fit in with the rest of the network infrastructure. We expand on all these principles in the following chapters. Although we cannot cover every aspect of these unique devices, we hope to describe those most-often used in your enterprise deployments.

Chapter 2

DataPower Quick Tour and Setup

In Chapter 1, "An Introduction to DataPower Appliances," we outlined what an appliance (specifically, a DataPower appliance) is and what it is used for. We focused that discussion primarily at the conceptual, more abstract level. Let's dive in and get our hands dirty. In this chapter, we take a closer look at the devices, and then show you what you should do to get up and running. We'll get started with the conventional, physical appliances and then discuss the setup and configuration of the virtual appliances.

Getting Started with Your New Appliance

It is not unlike many technical practitioners to be in a hurry to rip open and install new products as they arrive from the shipping dock. Certainly, lengthy corporate procurement processes can help to build the anticipation! And as we know, many in the technical space prescribe to the mantra "Documentation be damned!"

However, despite their reputation for simplicity, appliances like any other product should be carefully planned for and implemented to prevent later rework and reconfiguration. Let's take a walk through the process.

Hey Bert, Got a Package for You...

For those of us who get excited about technology, it's a great moment when the device finally arrives in its well-padded shipping container. The contents yield the following:

- DataPower appliance
- Rack-mount kit
- Power cords
- Connection cables
- Resource Kit CD
- Printed Installation Guide

The Installation Guide has the usual dire electrical warnings and other good advice such as not to use the appliance for a "shelf or workspace." (So you'll have to find another place for those potted plants and pictures of the kids.)

TIP—Read the ***** Manual!**

Although experience shows that folks often don't open up the manual, it's a good idea to temper your excitement for a few moments and read through the short Installation Guide, even though we take you through the process in this chapter.
Things like the rack space and cable/pinout requirements are important, but boring, so we won't repeat them here, and instead refer to the details in the guide.

The Resource CD has a great deal of valuable content that should also be examined, and some of the items found on it may have updated versions on the DataPower Web page. Although the contents of the CD change occasionally, some examples of what you might find follow:

- Installation Guide—This is a soft-copy of the printed install guide that comes in the box. We will refer to it often during the rest of this chapter!

- Features QuickStart Guide—This little-known document explains how to activate and where to get help for optional features you may have purchased. These include Application Optimization (AO), Database Connectivity (DC), Data Integration Module (DIM), IBM Security Access Manager (ISAM), Extended Oracle Support, and TIBCO (not all features area available on all appliances).

- Virtual Edition QuickStart Guide—For getting started with virtual editions, a guide for VMWare and one for Citrix.

- AO Files—Used to deploy AO connectivity to WebSphere Application Server or other remote hosts if you are using the AO option.

- Certificates for the WebGUI and remote XML management features—Used to install on other servers in order to accept SSL connections to these admin tools on the appliances.

- Drivers for the supplied cables.

- GatewayScript Files—Sample service patterns and test requests, referred to by the online documentation.

- Interoperability Service test clients and samples— We will discuss the Interoperability Service later in the book. It is used for testing flows through the appliances.

WARNING —Resource CD Certificates

The certificates that are mentioned above, which are included in the Resource CD, should not be used in production environments. The reason is simple security logic—every other DataPower customer has a copy of them!

The appliances are 1U or 2U rack-mountable devices. The Installation Guide has the specifics regarding exact size and weight, and the operating environment and power considerations. Because that information is readily accessible on the IBM product Web site, we won't repeat it here. Due to the devices' massive processing power, there is an array of fans to keep them cool. These are variable speed fans and may be somewhat louder at startup or reboot than during normal runtime in a climate-controlled area.

Let's inspect our newly acquired device. Figure 2-1 shows these components on the front of 9005 2U platform. As stated earlier, the 9006 is very similar—there are two hard drives rather than four and the console connector is moved next to MGT0/MGT1. The 9005 1U platform is the same externally as the 9005 2U shown, other than there are only four 1-gig Ethernet ports and two hard drive modules. The five menu buttons next to the LED display are inactive at this time, and reserved for future use. The fault LED lights up in amber to indicate a critical hardware event. The power button can be used to power up, perform a graceful shutdown (one press), or immediate shutdown (press for five seconds).

Unlike the older generations, you should use the MGT0/MGT1 ports for management only, not data! MGT0 supports IPMI over LAN as well as serial over LAN. The RJ45 console connector port takes the place of the DB9 serial interface port on the older appliances for initial configuration, and can be used with an ASCII terminal or PC running terminal emulation software. For those appliances with the optional Hardware-Security Module (HSM), there is no longer a need for a Pin Entry Device (PED) and no associated port on the appliance.

TIP—Using the Locate LED

Locate LED—what the heck is that for? Well, it can be illuminated in blue to 'locate' a specific appliance. Ever sit in the datacenter, connected to the WebGUI, and confused about which physical appliance in the rack you are configuring? Well, just go to Administration→Main→System Control and turn it on to see which appliance it is! Or, through CLI, use the locate-device on/off command.

On the 9005 1U, the four left-side 1-gig RJ45 Ethernet ports are ETH10-ETH13. On the 9005/9006 2U, there are eight and they are ETH10-ETH17. The right side of both types has two 10-gig small form-factor pluggable (SFP+) ports for

ETH20–ETH21. The SFP+ ports can use short or long reach transceivers or direct attach cables, providing fiber-optic support. On all Ethernet ports, the tiny LEDs at the bottom indicate speed and activity. The left bottom LED is for speed and is green for 1-gig connections, amber for 10-gig or higher. The right bottom LED will be steady green for linked status, and blinking when it that port is being accessed.

INFO—SFP+ Cables/Transceivers

SFP+ port use depends on the transceiver on the other end. Possibilities are fiber, copper, or direct attach copper (DAC). First check for switch compatibility, then use the same modules on the switch and appliance sides. DAC cables and transceivers are bundled together into the same unit, so in this case all you have to check is the compatibility of the DAC cable with the switch

The hard disk LEDs are configured to show activity and status. On the 9005 1U, the left hard disk activity LED will show green for an active drive, and green blinking to show activity. The right fault LED is nonfunctional. On the 9005/9006 2U types, the left activity LED functions the same as 1U, and the right fault LED will blink amber to indicate a failed drive. No LED illumination means the drive is not active.

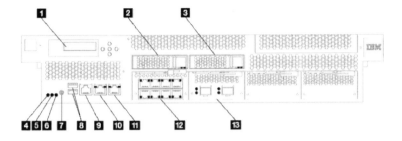

Figure 2-1 9006 IDG external components – 1) LCD Display 2) Hard disk drive 1 3) Harr disk drive 2 4) Fault LED 5) Locate LED 6) Power LED 7) Power button 8) Two USB ports (inactive) 9) Console connector 10) mgt0 management port 11) mgt1 management port 12) 1 Gb Ethernet module 13) 10 Gb Ethernet module.

The rear view is not as interesting, simply a bunch of fan modules and power supplies. The fan modules have LEDs too. If those are lit, there is a problem with the fan modules. The fans are variable-speed, so they will make more of a racket when they are starting up than they do in the normal running state, in a well climate-controlled data center. The hotter the internal temperature of the devices, the faster the fans will spin.

The power supply LEDs function as follows:

- If the LED is steady green, the appliance is connected to a power source working as designed.
- If the LED is blinking green once per second, the appliance is in standby mode (connected to a power source, but not turned on).
- If the LED is red and blinking three times per second, there is a problem with the module.

If the LED is dark, the module is not connected to power.

TIP-Important Resources Not in the Box

It's best to be aware of all possible resources when doing any kind of work so that if problems occur, you have places to turn for help. We've already discussed the resources that come with the product. There are also many others you should be aware of. These are listed for you in Appendix E, "DataPower Resources"

Next Steps—The Planning Phase

Before moving on to our next step, where you actually configure and enable the device, it is best to have some planning discussions with representatives from various areas of your IT department.

For example, the network team should be consulted for placement and integration with other network components, firewall ports that need to be opened, and other topics. You need the network team to assign one or more static IP addresses, depending on how many interfaces on the appliances you plan to enable. You need default gateways, possibly static routes, and other network-related information for the administrative ports and those that will carry message traffic.

If you plan on using SSL for network connections, you may need keys and certificates created by your security team or from outside sources. The application and security teams may have to describe what types of integration will be necessary for their applications.

If Web services endpoints will be looked up in a registry dynamically or LDAP servers need to be read for authentication, then ports may need to be open in the firewalls from DataPower to those servers so that the traffic can flow. Plan carefully and enlist the help of people on those teams!

Next Steps—What You Will Need

To do the initial configuration described in the next section, you need the following items (in addition to what came with the appliance):

- A copy of the Installation Guide – best to print this out and ensure you have the latest (Fifth Edition, April 2013 as of this writing).
- Network cables for all ports that you wish to configure (at least two).
- Supported terminal emulator software on your workstation; alternatively, an ASCII terminal.
- The RJ45 to DB9-F (female) serial console cable or RJ45 to USB console cable that was supplied with the appliance.
- Network information—one or more IP addresses, default gateways, subnet masks, DNS server info, NTP server IP/hostname, and static routes, as described above.
- Medium cross-tip (Phillips) screwdriver for rack mounting.
- Both power cables and an AC power source to plug the device into.

Connecting and Powering Up Physical Appliances

The Installation Guide has clear instructions and diagrams about the rack-mounting procedure. We don't want to use valuable space here repeating all of the mundane steps in the Installation Guide for hooking things up physically (rack/wiring/power), so we will refer you to it when necessary. It is our intent to provide you with additional guidance wherever possible. There are very good instructions and warnings about these topics in that document, so please read and heed!

Assuming the rack mounting has been done; let's get to the good part. Obviously, a good first step might be to connect the power cords. Do so according to the Installation Guide, but do not power on the appliance yet.

TIP—Power Connections

Whenever loss of data is a concern, you should have both power cords connected to independent, conditioned power sources. Those redundant power supplies are there for a reason! Failing to do so will result in blinking lights and repeated dire warnings in the DataPower log about a power supply having "failed" when, in fact, the problem is that it is not connected.

At this point, make your network cable connections, per the Installation Guide, for any network ports you wish to configure. To get started, at a minimum you will have to use the RJ45 to USB or RJ45 to DB9 serial cable to connect from the appliance (RJ45) console connector port (shown in Figure 2-1) to your ASCII terminal or workstation. You will also, at a minimum, want to configure MGT0 or MGT1 for administrative access from your network. If you will be using serial over LAN, you need to use MGT0.

TIP—Connect, Then Boot

On first initialization, you should always connect the serial cable first, and then power up the appliance. This enables you to see the boot sequence and any error messages that might appear during the boot process.

If you are using Windows®, you may want to verify which COM port the USB serial cable is using. To do this, go to Start→Computer, right-click, and then click on Manage. The Computer Management applet displays. Click on Device Manager and then open the Ports section. You should see your cable listed and the port it is using, as shown in Figure 2-2. If your workstation does not recognize the cable, there are instructions in the Installation Guide describing how to install the device drivers for Windows and Mac systems. The drivers are located on the Resource CD that is supplied with the appliance and available for download online.

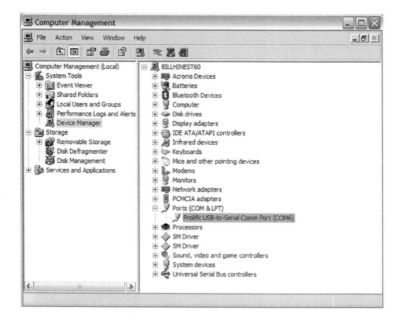

Figure 2-2 Checking the USB COM port.

Now it's time to get a terminal session established. Any ASCII terminal emulation software can be used for this (such as Putty), as the requirements are simple. Set the connection up with 9600 baud, 8 bits per character, no parity, 1 stop-bit, and no flow control.

You may now fire up the appliance using the power button on the front. You may notice that initially the fans are quite loud and then decrease in volume as the boot-up sequence progresses.

Installing and Configuring Virtual Appliances

Virtual edition is supported on a growing number of platforms, but for demonstration purposes we will use the ubiquitous VMWare ESX. The install/config on other platforms, including

VMWare Workstation for developer editions, will be very similar and these are documented on the IBM website as well.

TIP—Server/Workstation Virtualization Enablement

In order to use hardware-supported virtualization with products such as VMWare, you may need to change a BIOS setting on your server or workstation. For example, the 'Intel(R) Virtualization Technology' or 'VT –d Feature' BIOS settings might be at Advanced→Processor Configuration or under Config→CPU→Virtualization.

In your VMWare vSphere client, browse to the location of your DataPower Virtual Edition .ova file and choose File→Deploy OVA Template from the menu as shown in Figure 2-3, and click Next.

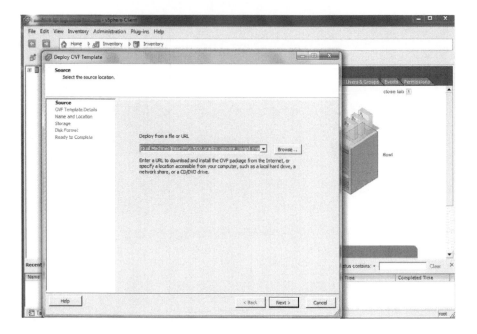

Figure 2-3 Select the DataPower Virtual Edition OVA file.

On the next pages, select the proper configuration for your host environment and usage, as shown in Figure 2-4. The OVF Template comes with three configurations.

- Small: 4 CPUs, 4 GB RAM, 4 NICs
- Standard: 8 CPUs, 8 GB RAM, 4 NICs
- Enterprise: 16 CPUs, 96 GB RAM, 4 NICs

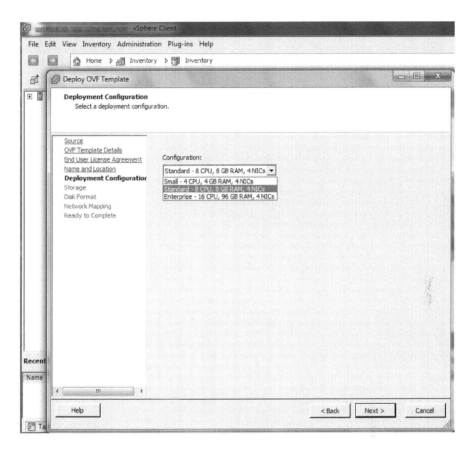

Figure 2-4 Selecting the Deployment Configuration.

On the next page, you must specify how you would like the disks provisioned. Thick provisioning allocates all the disk space in advance. Thin provisioning allocates minimal disk space and allows the space to grow as needed after deployment, up to the configured size. This is shown in Figure 2-5.

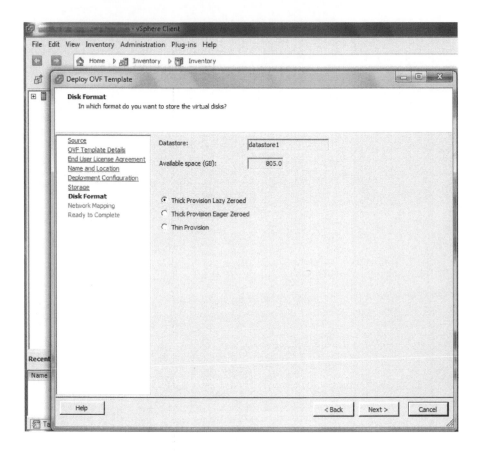

Figure 2-5 Selecting disk provisioning.

The next step is to configure the networks that the virtual environment should have access to. You must have created virtual switches in your network environment for handling traffic from the guests. See the VMWare vSphere Client documentation for how to create a virtual switch. This step is shown in Figure 2-6.

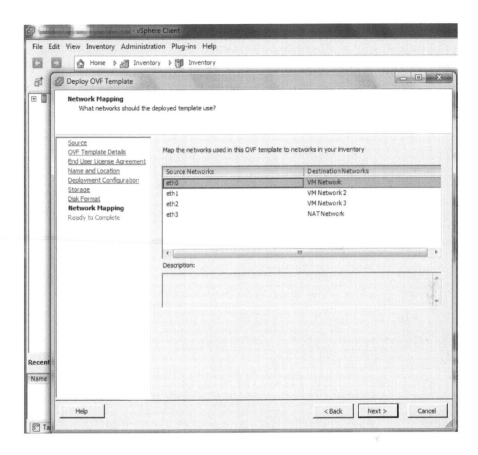

Figure 2-6 Configuring the virtual networks.

The network config in the Virtual Edition is a bit different than the physical appliances. First, there are no network speed restrictions introduced by the Virtual Editions. If the infrastructure supports 10 GbE, then it can be used by all visible virtual interfaces. Physical appliances have a defined number of interfaces, whereas the virtual appliances are limited to what is configured in the host environment (the documentation says there is a limit of four for virtual). These can however, all be 10 GbE if that is how the underlying host environment is configured.

TIP—Network Caveats

It should be obvious, but we'll state it here in order to be sure. If multiple virtual interfaces are using the same, singular 10GbE NIC, they will each run at less than 10 gig! Also, if the vSphere admins add or remove interfaces in the environment, this will obviously affect what is available to you in the DataPower network config. So if you have only two interfaces, and the 'Add' button is disabled, those are the folks to talk to.

From here, just review and click Finish to complete the installation, and wait while the progress bar indicates that everything is done (this can take a while). For those of you who prefer automated deployments, be aware that VMWare provides a command line tool called ovftool that allows the scripting of the installation. The rest of our DataPower configuration is done in the CLI command shell, as described in the following section.

Completing the Install in the CLI Shell

Our examples that follow will be using a virtual (software) XI52, so there may be minor differences if you are configuring a physical appliance (additional interfaces, etc). You should now see the text "DPOS boot – press <ESC> within 7 seconds for boot options..." followed by the boot-up sequence text. The "boot options" are actually a hardware diagnostic test that are performed if the <ESC> key is pressed during this time interval. It is intended to be used under the supervision of IBM support, and triggers additional logging and checks on the inventory of installed components, BMC/sensor, network, memory, and disks. When the boot-up sequence finishes, you should be presented with a login prompt. Log in as the built-in user 'admin' and provide the password from the Installation Guide. (OK, it's probably 'admin' as well.). You will be forced to change this password later in the process.

Next you must choose to enable or disable an operational mode, depending on which appliance you are initializing. Enter a 'y' to accept a mode or a 'n' to decline. The operational modes are as follows.

- Disaster Recovery Mode – if you enable this mode, you will later be able to create 'secure' backups of the entire appliance. Normal backups do not contain sensitive data, such as private keys and on-board account information. This would be dangerous, since they are not encrypted. Disaster Recovery mode allows you to do a full, encrypted backup that contains everything. There are additional steps to restore an appliance from that backup (you must have a copy of the private key to decrypt the backup). See Figure 2-7 for a screen shot of this process. Also note that if the appliance has the optional HSM card, the secure backup will not contain the private keys that are stored in the HSM module. When the secure restore is complete, the admin password will be reset to the default of 'admin'. This is to avoid issue of forgetting the admin password at the time of the backup.

- Common Criteria Mode – enforces a strict set of policies required to pass CCEAL4 evaluation. If you don't know what this is, and don't have a specific requirement to use it, then don't enable it! These options cannot be changed back without re-initializing the appliance.

```
the only way to change an operational mode is to reinitialize
the appliance.

Press any key to continue.
******************************************************************

Disaster recovery mode allows you to create a secure backup to recover the
configuration of an appliance. A secure backup contains private data from
the appliance, including certificates, keys, and user data.
You cannot see the data in the backup, for only a DataPower appliance can decryp
t the backup.

You should enable this mode to create secure backups for use after an
appliance failure or during end-of-life migration.

Enable Disaster Recovery mode? Yes/No [y/n]:n

Common Criteria places the appliance in a mode that
enforces a set of policies that is required to pass Common Criteria
security testing (EAL4).

If you are unsure about whether to enable this mode, you should probably
answer no.

Enable Common Criteria Compatibility mode? Yes/No [y/n]: n_
```

Figure 2-7 Prompt for Disaster Recovery Mode.

At this point, you should see the prompt to enter a new password. Watch your Caps Lock and Num Lock. As we stress in the tip that follows, safeguard this new password and do not lose it! The system will accept a trivial password. Of course, trivial passwords are not secure and dangerous, so follow your organization's normal password constraints.

TIP—Never, Ever Lose the Admin Password!

The admin password for the device is an important thing. If this password is lost and no other account with privileged access is configured, the only recourse is to send the device back to IBM to be reset. Of course, you may still log on to the device with other accounts that may have been created (we'll show you that step later), but there is only one admin superuser account. Safeguard that password carefully!

The next prompt asks if you want to run the Installation Wizard. Let's use that simple utility to complete the basics of our configuration, and then we will refine and complete the config using the browser-based WebGUI.

After indicating that you want to use the Installation Wizard, it will ask if you want to configure network interfaces. As you can see in Figure 2-8, the default answer is [y] so you can simply press the Enter key. It asks if you have all of the relevant information, and then if you wish to configure eth0. We will configure this one, as the choices for virtual DataPower are eth0-eth3. However, if you are configuring a physical appliance you may want to skip the ethx choice and move directly to configuring mgt0.

As shown in Figure 2-8, we are going to use DHCP for our simple example, since our goal is to perform the minimum configuration to get to the WebGUI to do the rest. However, if you already know the correct values for the IP address, subnet mask, and default gateway you should decline DHCP and enter those values. We then decline to configure the other interfaces, and move into configuring network services. Of these, we decline DNS and network identifier (to be configured later). Next we indicate that we want to configure remote services.

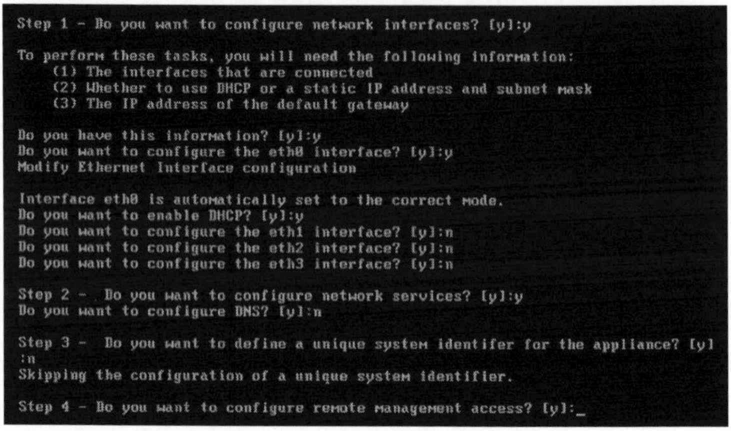

```
Step 1 - Do you want to configure network interfaces? [y]:y

To perform these tasks, you will need the following information:
     (1) The interfaces that are connected
     (2) Whether to use DHCP or a static IP address and subnet mask
     (3) The IP address of the default gateway

Do you have this information? [y]:y
Do you want to configure the eth0 interface? [y]:y
Modify Ethernet Interface configuration

Interface eth0 is automatically set to the correct mode.
Do you want to enable DHCP? [y]:y
Do you want to configure the eth1 interface? [y]:n
Do you want to configure the eth2 interface? [y]:n
Do you want to configure the eth3 interface? [y]:n

Step 2 -  Do you want to configure network services? [y]:y
Do you want to configure DNS? [y]:n

Step 3 -  Do you want to define a unique system identifer for the appliance? [y]
:n
Skipping the configuration of a unique system identifier.

Step 4 - Do you want to configure remote management access? [y]:_
```

Figure 2-8 Configuring the first Ethernet interface.

We will decline to configure SSH and telnet, but enable the WebGUI. To get started, and since we are using DHCP and don't know the IP address for eth0 yet, we are enabling the WebGUI across any configured interface. This is a temporary measure that we will fix later- keep in mind that systems should never be left in this state (see the TIP later). We use the default port of 9090 (some may consider this a security risk, especially for production systems, and choose to use a port that is not so well known and associated with the product). Figure 2-9 shows the remote interface config.

```
Step 4 - Do you want to configure remote management access? [y]:y

These configurations require the IP address of the local interface
that manages the appliance.

Do you have this information? [y]:
Do you want to enable SSH? [y]:n
Do you want to enable Telnet? [y]:n
Do you want to enable WebGUI access [y]:y
Enter the local IP address [0 for all]: 0
Enter the port number [9090]:
Modify Web Management Service configuration

Attention: If the password for the admin account is lost or forgotten,
you will have to delete the virtual machine. However, if another user
account can log in and if that account has the appropriate access
permission, that user can reset the password for the admin account.

Note: If you specify an existing user account, you will change the password
for this account.

Step 5 - Do you want to configure a user account that can reset passwords? [y]:_
```

Figure 2-9 Configuring remote access.

The next step is important. We warned you earlier that if you lose the built-in admin password, you may have to send the appliance back to IBM to be reset. The best way to avoid this (other than not losing that password) is to configure a second admin account as a privileged user. If the root admin password is lost, you can log in with this second account and change to the root admin password to a known value. Now don't go losing this password too, or you are back to the original problem! Figure 2-10 shows the configuration of the backup admin account.

```
account can log in and if that account has the appropriate access
permission, that user can reset the password for the admin account.

Note: If you specify an existing user account, you will change the password
for this account.

Step 5 - Do you want to configure a user account that can reset passwords? [y]:
Enter the name of the user account that can reset passwords [password-reset-user
]: admin2
New User configuration
Enter new password: *********
Re-enter new password: *********
Cleared RBM cache

Note: Configuration of the hard disk array is required to utilize the
hard disk array in this appliance.

Step 6 - Do you want to configure the hard disk array? [y]:y

This configuration requires the name of the file system to mount. Data in
this file system will be available in the local: directory.

Attention: This action destroys all data on the array volume.

Do you want to continue? [y]:_
```

Figure 2-10 Configuring the backup administrative account.

Following this step, we initialize the hard disk array, taking the default values for the file system name. On physical appliances, this can take a moment, so be patient. Figure 2-11 shows this configuration.

```
Note: Configuration of the hard disk array is required to utilize the
hard disk array in this appliance.

Step 6 - Do you want to configure the hard disk array? [y]:y

This configuration requires the name of the file system to mount. Data in
this file system will be available in the local: directory.

Attention: This action destroys all data on the array volume.

Do you want to continue? [y]:
Enter name for the file system [ondisk]:
Modify RAID Array configuration

File system successfully initialized.
Modify RAID Array configuration

File system successfully mounted.

Step 7 - Do you want to review the current configuration? [y]:_
```

Figure 2-11 Initializing the hard disk array.

You can now indicate to save the configuration (overwrite the previous config), and receive a message that the configuration is complete. In order to find out what IP address was assigned by DHCP to our eth0, we use the Command Line Interface (CLI) 'show int' command, as shown in Figure 2-12. If you are using the Virtual Edition, you can use the CLI command 'show hypervisor' to get details on the configuration (hypervisor name, edition, memory and CPU configuration of the guest, and UUID). We cover the CLI admin model in more detail later in the book, so in this chapter, we show you just enough to accomplish these goals. You may also use the DataPower CLI Command Reference as a guide.

```
idg# show interface

  interface         IP Address          RX (kb/pkts/errs)      TX (kb/pkts/errs)
  ----------        ----------          -----------------      -----------------
  lo                127.0.0.1           1169541/6892095/0      1169541/6892095/0

  gre0                                  0/0/0                  0/0/0

  sit0                                  0/0/0                  0/0/0

  ip6tnl0                               0/0/0                  0/0/0

  eth0              172.16.154.245      108504/784392/0        709963/4062082/0

  eth1              192.168.0.18        1195/13828/0           74/1159/0

  eth2                                  0/0/0                  0/0/0

  eth3                                  0/0/0                  0/0/0
```

Figure 2-12 Using the show interface command to see the network interface config.

When this is done, you should be at the main prompt, which shows as xi52(config)# for the XI52, as shown in Figure 2-12. You should type 'exit' and press the Enter key to exit configuration mode. You may want to leave this console session running, in case you do something wrong in the WebGUI and need to come back here to fix it. Now that you are through the preliminaries, our next objective is to finish the configuration using the WebGUI.

TIP—Be Sure to Use a Real IP Address

You cannot just guess at an IP address to assign to these interfaces. For example, you might find that your workstation is using 192.168.1.100 and think, "Well, I'll just use 192.168.1.500." IP addresses must conform to strict guidelines and be legitimate values in correlation with their subnet mask values. They must not be within the DHCP range for your network, or the DHCP server may give that same address out to another adapter on the network, causing an outage. You can use DHCP instead of a static IP address so that the appliances get an address dynamically at startup, but this is uncommon for server-type devices.

DataPower WebGUI Administrative Console Quick Tour

Now that we have enabled the WebGUI administrative console, we can use it for further changes. In your favorite supported Web browser, go to the address https://<ip_address>:<port>. We saw our IP address back in Figure 2-12. Notice that this is *https* rather than *http*.

Since the appliance uses a self-signed certificate by default, it's your web browser should will flag this as a security issue, since it does not have a corresponding certificate to validate it.

See the sidebar below for some comments about dealing with this issue.

The login page is shown in Figure 2-13.

Figure 2-13 Initial DataPower WebGUI login screen.

WARNING—Resource CD Certificates

To avoid the browser security warning about an untrusted SSL/TLS certificate being used for the WebGUI, you could either tell the browser to trust the certificate, or load it from the Resource CD into your browser's trust store, and the warning will go away. Keep in mind that it is always best to install your own certificates. The built-in ones are the same for every DataPower appliance. Using them means you will

*then trust <u>any</u> DataPower appliance, including a rogue one
that an attacker stands up to harvest passwords!*

You will notice that in addition to the typical user and password fields, there is a drop-down called "Domain." The only domain currently is called 'default'. Domains are areas of configuration isolation. They allow your configurations (which are in general proxies to backend applications) to be separated from each other (or grouped together) so that their environments can be independently restarted, backed up, administered, and so on. These are described in more detail in the "Device Administration" chapter in a later volume, where you will also learn how to create additional user and group accounts on the appliances.

For now, the only thing important related to domains is that the default domain should be used solely for global device configuration, and not for building application proxies. So, we log in to the default domain and continue our initial configuration. Enter the user admin and the new password that you created earlier, and press the Login button.

You are now presented with the Software License Agreement. This needs to be agreed to and accepted before doing anything else with the appliance. If you agree to the terms, press the "I agree" button. After you have done this, the system should ask you to log in again. You should also save the configuration now, using the Save Configuration link in the top right of the GUI, so that the license acceptance is permanent and you don't get prompted again.

Essential WebGUI Components

After logging in to the administrative console, the main page displays. This is broken into several main areas, as shown in Figure 2-14. In the upper-right corner, you can see the following:

- admin@<ip address:port>—This is a static text string indicating the currently logged in user and device name. Rather than a device name here, ours simply shows the IP address and port. We will fix that shortly.

- Domain—The domain that the current user is logged in to. You may move between domains simply by selecting another from this drop-down, as long as you have privileges to work in the domain you have selected.

- Save Configuration—As you make changes using the console, they are applied to the running configuration but are not saved to the persistent flash storage until you click this link.

- Logout—This logs the current user out of the console and returns to the login page.

Figure 2-14 WebGUI Control Panel.

TIP—Always Remember to Click Save Config

Configuration changes are not persisted until this button is clicked. If you do not save your changes and the box is recycled for any reason, your changes will be lost.

The bulk of the page is dominated by the Control Panel view, a series of categorized icons. You can see in Figure 2-14 that the icons are broken out into groups for Services (application proxies) that can be built, Monitoring and Troubleshooting tools, and File and Administration tools. To return to the Control Panel at any time, you can click the Control Panel link shown in the upper-left corner, which is present in all pages of the console.

On the left side of the page, below the Control Panel link, we find the link to the Blueprint Console. This is an area that has wizards and dialogs that will enable you to use the new patterns feature of DataPower, which features a rich new GUI. We will explore the Blueprint Console and patterns in a later volume of this book.

Below the Blueprint Console link is a search box. This powerful feature was introduced to quickly and easily find anything in the Navigation menu below it. It works great, and it's a big time saver, give it a try!

This leaves the final area of the console, which is the Navigation menu. Clicking any of these hyperlinked categories (Status, Services, Network, Administration, or Objects) opens up a contextual sub-menu. There is overlap in functionality between the Navigation menu and Control Panel—for example, you can select and edit a Web Service Proxy through either means; however, while the Control Panel often offers a more streamlined and wizard-like screen flow, the interface exposed by the Navigation menu may offer additional advanced options that are not visible through the Control Panel view of the same object (for example, the capability to enable or disable a configuration object).

Note the static text below the Navigation menu in Figure 2-14; this is a quick way to find out what model device and what firmware level the appliance you are currently logged in to is running, and also a handy hyperlink for DataPower support.

Let's explore the Navigation menu more. Clicking on the Status link opens up this section to an amazingly long sub-menu. It would be worthwhile to spend a lot of time here to get a feel for the types of things that can be monitored on the device. In most cases, these would be monitored by some external software, using SNMP or SOAP, but it's handy to be able to do a quick check using the WebGUI.

Two important items in the Status menu are at the top— the System Logs and Audit Log. The system log in the default domain shows logging activity for every domain on the appliance. It can be filtered down to show activity for specific domains, or for specific types of messages (for example, only log messages related to certificate expiry). The audit log shows when things such as maintenance to keys and certs, firmware changes, and device reboots are done and who did them. It shows all historical information until it reaches its maximum size, at which time a backup of the audit log file is stored on the file system and a new audit log file is created. See the chapter "Logging and Monitoring" in a later volume for more details on saving this log for historical data.

TIP—Separate Administrative Accounts

Being able to capture audit log activity is just one of many good reasons to have separate accounts for each person who will be administering the device. Similar to the root account and password for a Unix server, the admin account should rarely be used and the password for it known only to a few select people.

Completing the Configuration

Now that we have completed our initial network configuration and enabled the WebGUI, let's continue. Note that we have only configured one of the Ethernet interfaces available on the appliance. Certainly we will need more than just that one.

Completing the Network Config

We have configured the first management Ethernet interface using the Installation Wizard; now let's finish the network configuration within the WebGUI. You can change the DHCP-supplied IP information for a static one based on the input from your network team. If you do this, don't forget to re-enter the new address in your browser in order to get to the WebGUI at its new location!

For our example, we will enable a second interface for application (client) traffic. The network configuration can be changed only while in the default domain, which is where we still are because we haven't created any other domains. In Figure 2-15, we show the configuration page reached by *Network→Interface→Ethernet Interface→eth1*   in   the Navigation menu. We have entered the IP address for the interface to listen on and the default gateway. You would press the 'Apply' button to finish this configuration.

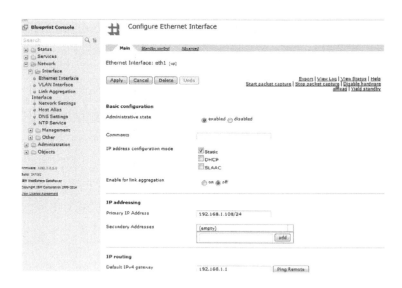

Figure 2-15 Configuring the eth1 network interface.

TIP—Never Use 0.0.0.0

Although many examples you may come across for enabling the WebGUI and other administrative interfaces on the device will show 0.0.0.0 being used as the listening IP address, we strongly urge you not to do this. This means that the appliance will listen on all configured interfaces on the device for administrative traffic. For example, you could access the WebGUI from the Ethernet interface designated for client traffic. It is a good security practice to segregate admin traffic from application traffic so that the rest of the world cannot discover your admin interfaces. You could argue that they would still need a password to do anything, but why allow them to get halfway there? Set up a management

interface and enforce strictly that all administrative traffic
flows through it.

The next step in our network setup configures the device
for DNS so that hostnames can be resolved. Under
Network→Interface→DNS Settings you can see a list of
configured servers. Clicking the Add button under DNS Servers
reveals the entry screen shown in Figure 2-16. We simply need
to provide the IP address of a DNS server here and accept the
other defaults to add it to the list.

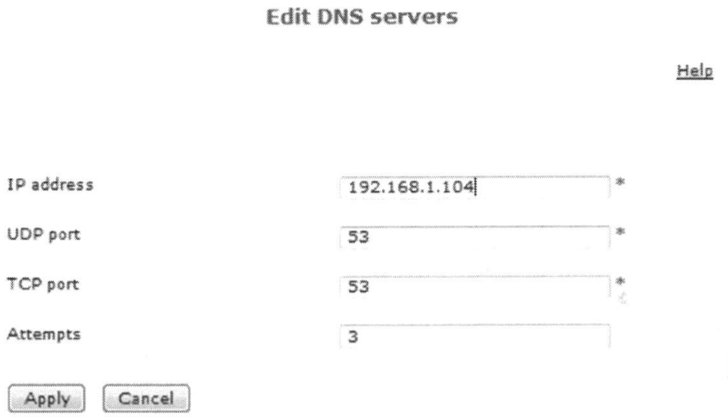

Edit DNS servers

Help

IP address	192.168.1.104 *
UDP port	53 *
TCP port	53 *
Attempts	3

Apply   Cancel

Figure 2-16 DNS server configuration.

To test the DNS config, you can go back to the Control
Panel and choose the Troubleshooting icon; on the resulting
page, you see a Ping tool, where you can enter a hostname such
as www.google.com and test to see whether it can be resolved
and reached by the device.

It is a recommended practice to configure host aliases for the network interfaces on the device. This helps to keep your configurations more portable, sort of like a built-in DNS name that the configuration uses, rather than propagating an IP address that could change later. We discuss this in more detail in the "Build and Deploy Techniques" chapter in a later volume. Figure 2-17 shows the two host aliases we built by going to *Network→Interface→Host Alias*.

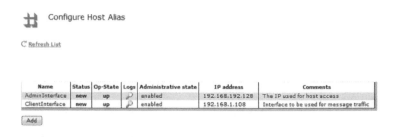

Figure 2-17 Host Alias configuration.

Let's look at how to take measures to ensure that the system date and time will remain correct. One common way to do this is to set computer systems in the network infrastructure to use NTP to tie them to some common central NTP server for synchronization. We highly recommend the latter approach, so that all components in the network infrastructure are synchronized. Disparities of even a few seconds between different participating components in a given transaction can wreak havoc and make troubleshooting and log correlation quite difficult.

Figure 2-18 shows how to do this by going to *Network→Interface→NTP* Settings, clicking the radio button to enable the service, providing the hostname or IP address of an NTP server, clicking the Add button, and then committing the changes. You should also go to *Administration→Device→Time Settings* to set the correct time zone for the geography in which the device will operate.

Figure 2-18 NTP configuration.

Let's continue with the Network menu to turn on the SSH Service so that we can do secure remote command line administration. As shown in Figure 2-19 (reached from *Network→Management→SSH Service*), we have clicked the Select Alias button to choose the AdminInterface host alias (rather than entering the IP address directly, or worse yet—0.0.0.0!) and then enabled the service with the radio button and clicked the Apply button. Notice in this figure that you can also enter an access control list of client IP addresses that are permitted to connect to the SSH service on the device. This is available for all administrative interfaces.

Figure 2-19 SSH configuration.

Similarly, the WebGUI settings can be tweaked. Figure 2-20 shows this configuration screen, reached from *Network→Management→Web Management Service*. This was already enabled in our Install Wizard session, but we have switched the earlier (non-secure) 'any interface' 0.0.0.0 IP address setting to our new host alias. If you feel that the timeout value is too short, and you are being forced to repeatedly log in, you can also extend the timeout value here. Be aware that longer values mean less security!

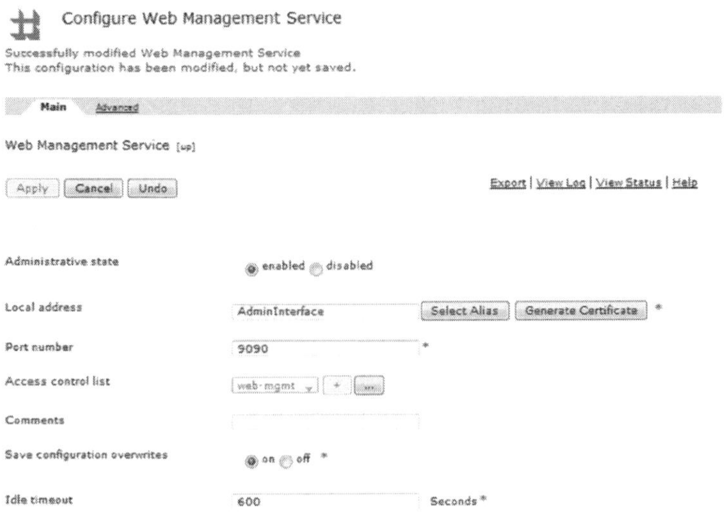

Figure 2-20 WebGUI configuration.

TIP—WebGUI Idle Timeout Values

Be careful with this value. The default is 600 seconds, or 10 minutes. Extending this value means you are decreasing security (for example, in the event someone leaves their workstation unlocked while logged in). While extending this may be acceptable in some development environments, we suggest never using the setting of zero, which means no timeout. When a user logs out (or is timed out), resources such as temp file space are freed up on the device for efficiency. For as long as it takes for that to happen, those resources will continue to accumulate.

The last stop in the Network menu is to turn on the XML Management Interface (discussed in the "Alternate Management Interfaces" chapter in a later volume). As you may have guessed by now, this is reached by *Network→Management→XML Management Interface*. Here, you simply specify the AdminInterface host alias again, and enable the service as we have done for SSH and the WebGUI.

We will do one last bit of housekeeping before we move on. In Figure 2-14, we said that we could customize the device name, and this would show on the console page rather than the IP and port. Here's how you set that. Figure 2-21 shows the configuration from *Administration→Device→System Settings*. Now you can see where that customized device name shown on the login page is set. See Appendix A, "DataPower Naming Conventions" for some ideas about naming the system and other configuration artifacts.

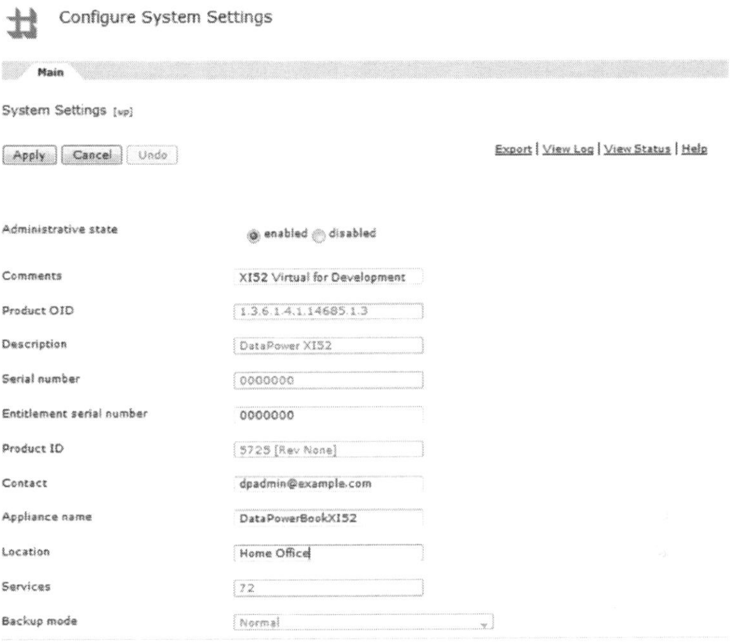

Figure 2-21 Customized system settings.

You may also notice the ability to add a "Custom User Interface File" on this same page. This feature expands on the capability to add a "welcome message" on the WebGUI page in earlier firmware versions. By editing the custom user interface XML file, you can provide custom text for CLI command prompts and pre-login, post-login, and other appliances messages (for example, "This is the production system; make changes with care!") for both the CLI and the WebGUI, and also color code those messages on the WebGUI. This feature is well documented, and it is highly recommended to take advantage of it to reduce the chance of administrators making changes to the "wrong" system!

Backing Up the System

Before we take our last step (update the firmware), let's back up the system configuration. Even though firmware updates should not affect your configuration in any way, this is always a good idea before making major changes or updates to any computer system.

With DataPower, this is simple to do. Figure 2-22 shows that we have gone to *Administration→Configuration→Export Configuration* and chosen to back up the entire system. Clicking the Next button here takes you to a page that enables you to enter a backup name (this should be something descriptive such as exportFullMyXI52_Init_Config_<date>) and any comments you want to add.

DataPower appends the .zip extension to whatever filename you give it, so don't include it in the filename. Clicking the Next button on that page results in a brief pause, and then a page appears with a Download button to enable you to download the backup zip file to your workstation. For flexibility and redundancy, you may also want to make a separate backup of just the default domain (although this information is included in a full system backup).

Note that this really isn't a backup of the 'entire' system. If you chose the Disaster Recovery Mode back when we first initialized the appliance, you can use secure backup/restore option to create an encrypted backup with sensitive information such as private keys, certificates, and on-board user passwords. The backup file is secured using an appliance public and private key and can only be restored with the same key pair. Note that if the appliance has the optional HSM card, the secure backup will not contain the private keys that are stored in the HSM module.

Figure 2-22 Backing up the appliance.

TIP—Secure Backup/Restore

It's important to note that Secure Backup is not a migration tool, as it can't be used between different firmware levels. You must restore to the same firmware level that the backup was taken on. There is a manifest file in the backup set that identifies the firmware it was taken on. We recommend that a common single secure backup key/cert is used for all appliances at a site. The admin ID is reset back to the default password during a secure restore. See http://www.ibm.com/developerworks/websphere/library/te charticles/1009_furbee/1009_furbee.html for additional details.

Updating the Appliance Firmware

The final step in the initial configuration of the device is typically to upgrade the firmware from whatever level was installed in the factory to the latest level. This is a best practice, since quite often the firmware shipped in the appliance does not contain he latest fixes. First, check to see whether you are already up to date. You saw in Figure 2-14 how to quickly see what version you have. Also, go to *Administration→Device→System Settings* and take note of your machine type.

Next, you need to go to the IBM DataPower Fix Central Web site and check the available firmware levels to see whether there are newer ones. If so, download the firmware file that corresponds to the features that you purchased with your appliance. If you aren't sure, you can check by going to *Status→System→Device Features*, which shows which licenses are enabled for this device. Do not confuse this with the similarly named menu choice *Status→System→Library Information*, which shows which features are actually installed on the device firmware. For instance, you may have purchased the Tivoli Access Manager feature and have that license enabled on your appliance, but if you install a firmware image without it, then it will not actually be installed. (This can always be fixed by downloading a firmware image with that feature.)

Our particular XI52 virtual appliance used for these examples started at version 7.0.0.0 and has licenses for all features except TIBCO, since it is a non-production version (these licenses are included for free in developer and non-production editions). From the download site, we have obtained file xi7001.scrypt4. The filename begins with "xi", designating that it is for an XI52, then continues with the firmware version (7001 meaning 7.0.0.1), and then the scrypt4 extension, which designates the firmware meant for virtual editions. Firmware for the physical appliances has the .scrypt3 extension.

Now that this update is on our workstation, we will move to *Administration→Main→System Control* in the Control Panel to do the update. First click the Save Configuration button to ensure that any changes we have made thus far are written to the flash.

There are three steps to the firmware upgrade process:

1. Upload the new firmware file.

2. Reload the current firmware.

3. Boot the new image.

Figure 2-23 shows the first step of this process. In this figure, the Upload button has already been used to bring the firmware file up to the device. The uploaded firmware update file is now shown in the drop-down list. Now select Reload Firmware in the Shutdown section and press the Shutdown button. There will be a brief pause, and you will be returned to the login page.

Log back in to the device and return to *Administration→Main→System Control*. Reselect the uploaded firmware image in the Boot Image section, check the box accepting the license agreement (if you do in fact accept the term) and then press the Boot Image button. We do mean a few minutes, so be patient!

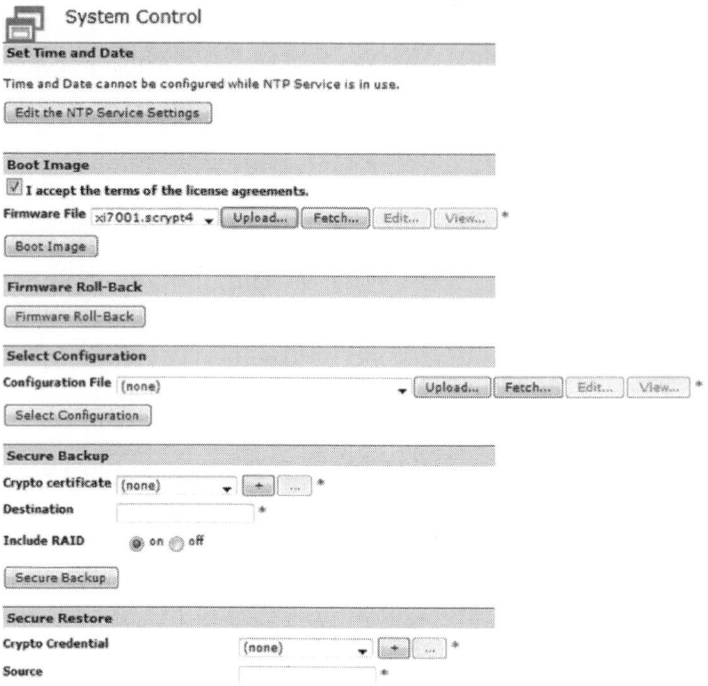

Figure 2-23 Uploading the firmware update file.

While this is typically much faster than a standard server reboot, there is a lot of intensive action going on behind the scenes. Finally, reboot the appliance (you are prompted at these steps to click an OK button) and then you should be able to load the login page again.

We think you will agree—this is much faster and simpler than updating the software on a typical server! Figure 2-24 shows that our appliance has now been updated to version 7.0.0.1. It also shows the new name that we have given to the appliance—DataPowerBookXI52.   You   may   also   want   to capture another backup at this point.

NOTE—Alternate Methods of Updating Firmware

It may be preferable to upgrade the firmware from the CLI command shell (which is covered in the Alternate Management Interfaces chapter), as it is an intensive operation for a browser-based interface, and the CLI would provide more feedback during the process. There is a detailed technote available on the DataPower support page with instructions on how to do this. Another approach would be to use the WebSphere Appliance Management Center. As discussed in our later chapter on managing multiple devices, this utility applies firmware updates across a managed set of devices in a controlled manner.

Figure 2-24□Firmware update completed.

TIP—Powering Down the Appliance

While it is rare, any time you need to power down the appliance, it is a good practice to bring the system to a graceful halt first. To do this, save your configuration, select "Halt System" from the Mode drop-down, and then click the Shutdown button. A major advantage of this approach is that you are warned if there are unsaved configuration changes. You can also depress the physical power button to do a graceful shutdown (holding it down five seconds or longer will do an immediate, non-graceful shutdown).

Summary

In this chapter, we have shown you the process of unpacking a brand new device all the way through the initial configuration and prep, including a full backup. We have toured the physical characteristics of the appliance, as well as taken a spin through the main functional areas of the Web administration console. We have enabled two Ethernet interfaces for administrative and client use, performed the initial network configuration, and enabled the SSH and XML Management administrative interfaces. Not bad work for our first hands-on chapter! The next chapter, Chapter 3, "Common DataPower Deployment Patterns" will discuss some common usage patterns in the network. In Volume II, "DataPower Networking," we will further explore the network capabilities of the device.

Chapter 3

Common DataPower Use Cases

DataPower appliances originated during the early days of XML, where acceleration was the key requirement and then naturally transitioned to Web services and service-oriented architectures (SOA). They solved a very difficult problem - accelerated parsing and transformation of XML data with purpose-built compilers, parsers and crypto acceleration. DataPower was deployed to solve many security and integration uses cases using a configuration-based approach with extensibility using XSLT.

In today's world, where businesses must provide an enhanced digital experience to their customers, they need to solve similar security and integration challenges, but for different channels and with its own unique set of requirements. DataPower capabilities have evolved from SOA to provide robust support for mobile, API, Web, B2B and cloud workloads. The underlying value proposition remains the same, purpose-built appliances that combine superior performance with hardened security. For this reason, DataPower appliances have been strategically deployed at the edge of the network and are often referred to as 'gateway' devices. They are the entry point for your internal or external consumers across different channels whose message structures are different. These messages could be either XML or JSON, and secured using WS-Security or OAuth. This is what makes DataPower unique - it is a single multi-channel gateway platform to secure, integrate, control and optimize delivery of workloads across channels including mobile, API, Web, SOA, B2B and cloud.

This chapter will explore the various deployment patterns across the different channels to explain how to maximize your DataPower investment for a multi-channel enterprise. There are certain ways to do things that are generally seen as "always correct." However, this doesn't actually mean "always." There is no such thing as a "best" practice, because each and every deployment is different, and there cannot be a single answer that is the best for everyone! There are, however, certain ways of doing things that have been done time and time again, and each time they are done, they have worked because they make sense. In IT, we refer to these as "patterns"—recurring deployment scenarios that can be reused in similar circumstances to give a similar positive result. This chapter describes some common DataPower deployment patterns— things that have worked well for other DataPower customers, and most likely will work just as well for you!

Deployment Topologies

A common DataPower misconception is that appliances have a single use or purpose. This might be true for your common garden-variety kitchen appliances but certainly not for DataPower. Whereas a dishwasher is only good for one thing—

washing dishes—a DataPower appliance is adaptable and flexible. If it were a household appliance, it would wash your dishes, clean your clothes, vacuum your carpets, and mow your lawn—and it would do it as well, if not better than your existing appliances!

Okay, DataPower isn't really going to metamorphose into a robot and go trimming your hedges (feel free to submit an Enhancement Request). However, note that each of the tasks mentioned has a completely different setting, depending on the appliance. It would require a single appliance that is just as good in the kitchen as in the garden, in the utility room as in the bedroom. In each area, there are different specific tasks that need to be carried out and carried out well. Imagine if they could all really be carried out by a single appliance that could be easily repurposed or reconfigured to perform whatever task was at hand.

DataPower is an amazingly flexible combination of hardware and firmware in a consumable form that is able to solve many extremely difficult problems. It is precisely because of this flexibility that DataPower appliances are often deployed in completely different parts of an enterprise, performing completely separate roles. Deployments cover everything from security protection and application level firewalling to providing interoperability between disparate and incompatible systems to mediation and routing of messages. These are difficult challenges in today's changing enterprise landscape that can be solved using a single configurable appliance instead of multiple complex software products that are difficult and expensive to install, deploy, and maintain. Figure 3-1 shows some of the common DataPower use cases that are currently being used in many production environments across different geographies, industries, and different security networks (DMZ and trusted zone). We will expand on these patterns for the remainder of the chapter.

INFORMATION—Network Zones

DMZ (demilitarized zone) is a segment of the network that exposes enterprises services to an external untrusted network such as the Internet.

Trusted zone is a segment of the network that is protected from untrusted access, typically behind network firewalls. Access is only permitted from known network stations.

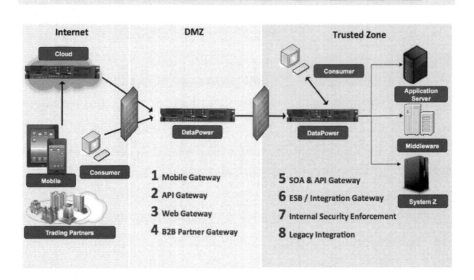

Figure 3-1 Common Deployment Patterns

DataPower as Mobile Gateway

The growth of enterprise mobility introduces a new set of security, integration and performance challenges. Access to data needs to be provided in a secure format that is consumable on mobile devices and where network bandwidth is not guaranteed. Furthermore, backend data may exist on heterogeneous systems and requires both message and protocol level integration. Some of these requirements are likely triggering a "deja-vu" moment – you were probably asked similar questions in your SOA journey, but instead of Web services, the architecture is now based on REST/JSON. The great news is that the same platform that powered your Web services workloads can also secure and optimize your mobile applications, providing security, integration and optimization of JSON messages, including full support for OAuth 2.0, which is a security protocol for providing third-party web and mobile applications secure access to resources.

DataPower Gateway appliances provide mobile gateway functionality that supports RESTful architectures, allowing you to configure different policy rules based on HTTP verbs. JSON payloads are optimally parsed for enhanced performance and enhanced security with built-in support for JSON threat protection, JSON schema, JSON Web Encryption, JSON Web Signature, JSON Web Token and JSON Web Key. Several options exist to natively transform JSON messages. Firmware V6 introduced support for JSONiq, which provides JSON extensions on top of XQuery. And let's not forget about GatewayScript–which provides a highly optimized and secure gateway programming model to enrich your mobile workloads within a DataPower processing policy flow. All of those gems in our processing policy, such as dynamic routing, and schema validation are still relevant for mobile use cases, so you can combine the new REST/JSON functionality with existing policy actions to still deliver the same robust capabilities for your mobile applications!

DataPower Gateways can easily integrate with mobile application platform such as IBM MobileFirst, which complements DataPower user and message security to provide mobile application management functionality (application authenticity, mobile application versioning, device single-sign-on (SSO) and more). This integration allows DataPower to be deployed in the DMZ in front of the IBM MobileFirst server to offload access management and provide gateway value-add functionality, such as message-level security, control and performance enhancements.

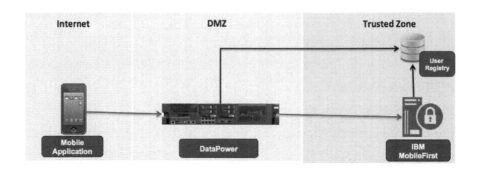

Figure 3-2 DataPower and IBM MobileFirst

The ISAM module on DataPower provides advanced access management capabilities for Web and mobile applications. This capability delivers a robust reverse proxy component that enforces multi-factor authentication using one-time passwords on mobile devices, context-based access from mobile devices using attributes such as geolocation, and facilitates mobile SSO to allow multiple applications to share login sessions on the same mobile device. The reverse proxy requires ISAM for Mobile for these scenarios, which provides policy authoring and policy-decision point for each access request. This allows you to visually build policies without any coding and easily enforce them using the reverse proxy on DataPower Gateways.

Figure 3-3 depicts the various components.

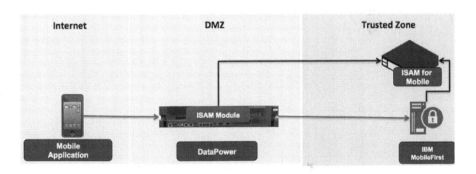

Figure 3-3 DataPower and IBM Security Access Manager

DataPower as API Gateway

You have probably heard the phrase, "data is the new oil." If it can save us trips to the gas pump then we will invest money into that data stock! Enterprises are providing managed access to their data via Internet-accessible API services, to allow third-party applications to build solutions without requiring custom integration logic and business contractual arrangements.

Technically speaking, APIs are either REST services using JSON or Web service using SOAP, both over HTTP(s). Special care must be taken to expose these services for public or private consumption. Enterprises need to provide self-service registration and documentation to API services using developer portals and control access to these services from known consumers. There are many examples of mobile applications that use API services. For example, say your favorite restaurant app, which show your Facebook friends who have visited a restaurant, Twitter hashtags of meals, Google Maps for directions, and many more. Mobile apps are using APIs to provide a better user experience for their users with social data (e.g. Facebook and Google APIs) or provide additional functionality to their customers (e.g. Pay with PayPal widget). API providers are exposing APIs to the public as a "product" for financial benefit or free to increase brand recognition, all in a tightly controlled manner. Many enterprises are also leveraging APIs for internal use across different lines of business to increase developer productivity and provide increased visibility of available internal services.

If you are itching to start participating in the API economy then pack your bags and get ready to begin your journey into the API economy, taking with you a familiar friend, your IBM DataPower Gateway appliance! If you already have DataPower appliances, you can use it is an API gateway as part of IBM API Management product. This solution consists of two components: a management appliance consisting of an API manager, developer portal and environment console, and IBM DataPower Gateway appliance as the API gateway runtime.

It allows you to easily manage APIs - design, secure, control, publish, analyze & manage using the API manager and publish into a developer portal for self-service consumption into developer communities. API owners can use the collected API analytics to analyze their APIs and make changes. Furthermore, it allows you to quickly provide API governance for API services – service versioning, lifecycle and documenting API consumer and providers. For more information about IBM API Management, I suggest you check out their developer site at https://developer.ibm.com/apimanagement/.

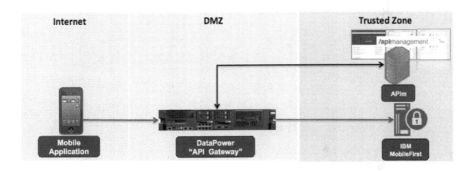

Figure 3-4 DataPower and IBM API Management

DataPower as Web Gateway

IBM DataPower Gateways have historically provided Web gateway capabilities to secure Web applications using either a Web Application Firewall or Multi-Protocol Gateway service. The addition of the ISAM proxy module on DataPower provides even greater Web reverse proxy functionality with advanced session management and URL rewriting. The ISAM reverse proxy is very reputable within the industry; it is deployed by a large number of customers worldwide and is the Web gateway for many mission-critical Web applications.

Using IBM DataPower Gateway appliances as a Web gateway allows you to consolidate infrastructure, provides cost savings, and simplifies your infrastructure by providing a single entry point for all your workloads. Furthermore, you can enrich your Web workloads with DataPower functionality, such as:

- Enforcement of service level agreement: Service-Level monitoring (SLM) to enforce rate limit between consumer and provider either based on transaction rates or backend latency.

- Workload optimization (self-balancing and intelligent load balancing to backend application servers): Deploy DataPower appliances in an active-active setup without an external load balancer and route to backend applications servers based on real-time metrics such as CPU utilization.

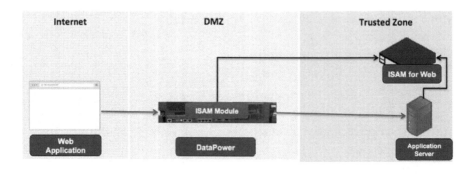

Figure 3-5 DataPower and IBM Security Access Manager for Web workloads

DataPower as B2B Partner Gateway

The DataPower XB62 appliance or B2B module on the IBM DataPower Gateway provide hardened B2B security in the DMZ or at the edge of your trusted zone. DataPower supports several key B2B messaging protocols, such as AS1/AS2/AS3/ebMS, and file transfer protocols (FTP, SFTP, SMTP/POP). You can easily manage and connect to trading partners for B2B governance, access control, message filtering, and data security. B2B protocols have non-repudiation requirements once the synchronous communication is completed. Quite often for regulatory requirements, B2B partners must be able to prove that messages were sent and received. The B2B transaction viewer on DataPower provides the ability to correlate documents and acknowledgments for all associated events, providing a persistent store that proves that messages were delivered and received.

DataPower B2B capabilities complement B2B messaging and commerce systems by acting as a B2B gateway in the DMZ, offloading partner connectivity and security functions. This combination allows you to easily scale when transactional volumes increase and quickly onboard trading partners.

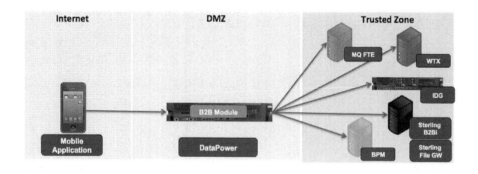

Figure 3-6 DataPower and B2B

DataPower as SOA Gateway

The most popular deployment pattern in production environments today is DataPower usage as a SOA gateway or Enterprise Service Bus (ESB). Many of DataPower core capabilities originated in the SOA world and are continuously been enhanced to meet the latest security standards. DataPower supports SOAP and WSDL standards to provide a common messaging and service interface language to allow interoperability between different Web service consumer and providers. The Web services security standards, such as WS-Security (or within WS-Policy wrappers) provide guidance on enforcing message integrity using XML Digital Signatures, message confidentiality using XML Encryption, and security assertions using various security token formats such as Security Assertion Markup Language (SAML), Kerberos, X509 certificates, and username tokens.

Transformation of SOAP/XML payloads is done using XSLT, which provides a highly extensible and performance engine to support concurrent transformations of various sizes.

This is the "secret sauce" of DataPower which has allowed to scale to handle the mission-critical transactions that power many of your banking, insurance, healthcare, auto, and government services (to just name a few of the relevant industries!)

DataPower easily integrates with WebSphere Service Registry and Repository to provide SOA governance, service lifecycle, versioning, endpoint management, and service-level authoring (e.g. define traffic levels for gold, silver and bronze consumers), which are authored in WSRR and pushed to DataPower for runtime enforcement. When compared to API management, WSRR provides governance across different service providers – MQ, Enterprise JavaBeans (EJBs) or CICS services with the ability to add metadata unique to your enterprise requirements. IBM API management focuses on API governance and integrates with WSRR to import service interfaces for exposing Web services as APIs.

Figure 3-7 shows a common deployment pattern with DataPower, WSRR and API management.

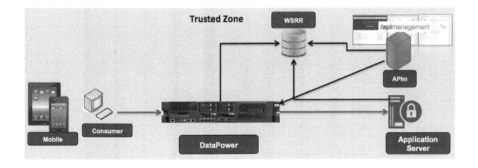

Figure 3-7 DataPower and WSRR

DataPower as Cloud Gateway

We have discussed many common use cases where DataPower Gateways are used today. These use cases assumed DataPower was running on-premise, within your data centers. In today ever-changing IT landscape, enterprises of all sizes are looking to leverage the economies of cloud to quickly build innovation solutions at lower costs. Enterprises are moving workloads or even their entire infrastructure into cloud environments, such as IBM SoftLayer, Amazon Web Services, Microsoft Azure, and more.

Cloud environments like SoftLayer provide hosting services where servers are deployed with an optimal set of resources and managed by the cloud provider. It's likely you have been using a Web site deployed on the cloud without even knowing it! That is one of the main benefits of cloud—you can move your workloads into the cloud and it will remain transparent to your users; furthermore, you will save infrastructure costs and gain the elasticity benefits of the cloud (dynamically scale the number of servers up during peak volume periods).

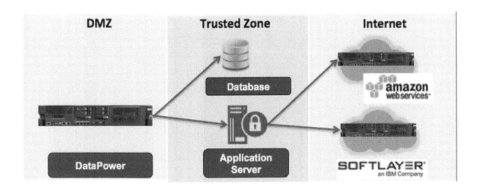

Figure 3-8 DataPower and Cloud Deployment

Security and integration requirements are going to be even more important when you deploy workloads on the cloud since you have less control over the infrastructure and running in public cloud environments requires an additional level of security. DataPower Gateways are well suited to meet the security and integration challenges for cloud workloads. You can use DataPower natively-built capabilities to protect messages with multi-factor authentication, message-level security, and robust transport-level security. DataPower Gateways can be deployed on SoftLayer bare metal servers with your choice of hypervisor (VMWare or Xen). This option gives you the most control over the deployment since you have dedicated access to the underlying server and can tune CPU, memory, and disk for each virtual machine instance. The deployment of DataPower on bare metal servers is similar to deploying using your on-premise hypervisor systems—the advantage of bare metal servers is that you don't need to manage the hardware.

Although there are cost savings to leveraging hardware in the cloud, one of the biggest advantages gained is using the cloud provider virtual server infrastructure. This approach does not provide you a dedicated server but it allows the cloud provider to deliver a highly-available environment and scale server resources to meet peak volumes. In Firmware V7.2, DataPower Gateway Virtual Edition is supported on virtual servers for SoftLayer CloudLayer Computing Instance (CCI) and Amazon Elastic Compute Cloud (EC2) servers. These deployment options provide increased flexibility and allow easier administration. You simply work with the DataPower Web GUI and do not need to worry about managing the hardware and server since the cloud provider manages them for you!

Industry regulations and data privacy concerns are one of the biggest hurdles that must be overcome to adopt public cloud technologies. Hybrid cloud integration is becoming a common pattern to provide secure access to sensitive data hosted within enterprise data centers from public cloud platforms. This "Hybrid Cloud," where one part is external and the other part is internal, poses unique security challenges. The Secure Gateway service on DataPower Gateways firmware V7.2 provides secure connectivity exclusively between IBM Bluemix (IBM Platform as a Service (PaaS) cloud platform) and on-premise enterprise applications protected using DataPower. This functionality will provide enhanced hybrid cloud integration, being able to gain the flexibility and cost benefits of running workloads on Bluemix, while still having secure access to sensitive data hosted within on-premise systems. The Secure Gateway service uses a layered approach to security with TLS and IP filtering. You don't need additional firewall rules to provide secure connectivity and can simply leverage existing enterprise firewall rules to enable quick connectivity. The Web GUI provides statistics for health monitoring and management of connections.

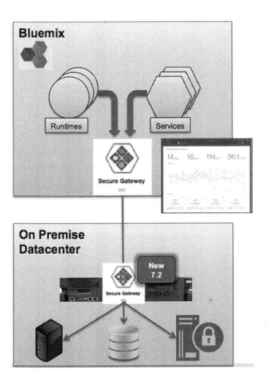

Figure 3-9 DataPower and Secure Gateway Service

The same security and integration challenges are going to exist and likely increase when you move your workloads to the cloud. IBM DataPower Gateways provide a multi-channel cloud gateway solution to protect your cloud workloads. You can easily deploy IBM DataPower Gateway virtual edition on supported cloud platforms and use the breadth of DataPower functionality powered by our natively-built platform and optimized DataPower Operating System.

DataPower as Security Gateway

In this chapter so far, we have talked about DataPower as a multi-channel gateway to secure and optimize workloads across mobile, API, Web, SOA, and B2B channels. A common usage for DataPower across these channels is security; hence DataPower is quite often coined as a "security gateway."

So, what is a security gateway? It is a hardened security proxy that sits at the perimeter of your environment, terminates incoming connections, ensures that the requests are "safe," and passes them on into your service provider or intermediary systems. An example of a security gateway deployment pattern is depicted below.

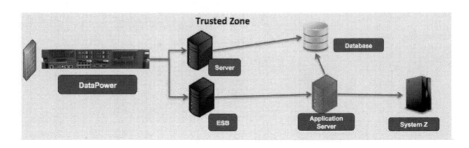

Figure 3-10 DataPower security gateway

IP firewalls simply restrict source/destination host and port numbers. DataPower Gateways provide additional level of protection on top of typical IP firewall capabilities. For example, a mobile application that sends a JSON request to a server on port 443 will pass straight through an IP packet firewall but it does not check the application layer content at all. This request may contain malicious content within the payload and can only confidently be examined using an application-level security gateway.

DataPower is a perfect fit for this type of deployment. The device is designed from the ground up for security and can be deployed into the DMZ without qualms. Moreover, you can use it to ensure that requests are "safe" at multiple levels, including parsing the XML or JSON to ensure that there is no malicious or accidentally dangerous content for backend software parsers calling out to external virus scanners via the ICAP protocol, schema validation, and authenticating, authorizing, and auditing the requests.

This level of protection is necessary in security devices. It deals with much more than the packet and protocol layers; it is up at the application layer, OSI levels 5 through 7, dealing with message content. By actually parsing and processing the content, DataPower in the role of a security gateway can protect against a class of real and increasingly sophisticated attacks. Let's take a slightly deeper look at some of these functions and answer the question: What role does DataPower actually perform when deployed in each of these situations?

SSL/TLS Termination

The decision on where to terminate SSL connections is an important decision for any Internet-accessible application environment. The SSL endpoint must be a secure hardened box with the capability to process the SSL handshake without detriment to performance, and the capability to proxy incoming connections to backend servers. DataPower uses dedicated cryptographic hardware and, among the SSL/TLS processing options are:

Handling client certificate authentication and specifying which SSL signers to trust

- Specifying SSL/TSL version and renegotiation
- Processing all the attributes in an SSL certificate to identify the owner
- Checking Certificate Revocation Lists
- Encryption algorithms to use (e.g. Elliptical Curve Technology – ECC)
- Prevent past security exposures with perfect forward secrecy (PFS)
- Use Server Name Indication (SNI) for multi certificate server name hosting

The inbound HTTPS connection from the client is terminated at DataPower. Messages are then processed on the device using the processing policy. Then the messages are sent on to the backend server. Note that the connection to the backend is likely to be over HTTPS (or any of the other supported backend protocols); however, this is a completely separate and independent SSL session to that of the client connection.

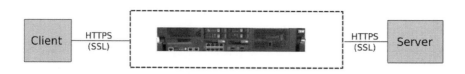

Figure 3-11 SSL Connectivity

Even when SSL is not in use, DataPower still acts as a connection termination point, ensuring that messages can never pass by without being inspected and deliberately routed onward.

Authentication and Authorization

Perimeter security is an increasingly common requirement for complex customer environments. DataPower can authenticate credentials for incoming requests and make authorization decisions based on those credentials and the resources requested. This can be done in many ways, including out of the box integration with enterprise authentication and authorization services and using many different standards.

Enterprise Single-Signon (SSO)

When consumers authenticate, they do so in a myriad of different ways. There are many different types of enterprise tokens, such as Security Assertion Markup Language (SAML), Lightweight Third-Party Authentication (LTPA), JSON Web Token (JWT), WS-Security custom binary token, and then even more possibilities beyond the standards. But what do we do if our consumer wants to provide one type of token, but our provider can only accept another type? Enter DataPower.

DataPower, sometimes in conjunction with another token transformation engine such as Tivoli Federated Identity Manager or other external authentication services, has the capability to mediate the communication between consumer and provider to map tokens from one kind to the other. The number of tokens supported out of the box is impressive and combined with the advanced cryptographic functionality on the device and the options for customization, the device can support a wide variety of token transformations.

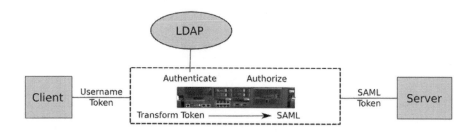

Figure 3-12 Authentication and SSO

For example, the client sends a request containing an OAuth access token, however the backend server only understands an LTPA token. DataPower can validate the access token; perform an authorization check on the resource, and then transform the token into an LTPA token —such that the backend server can understand it.

XML/JSON Threat Protection

It's a little known fact that even the most modern software parsers can be tricked cleverly with maliciously written well-formed XML or JSON messages that will use system resources leading to systems going down or even remote system compromise. The same symptoms can also be induced by simple application coding mistakes. The problem is that, by their nature, software parsers have to use up a huge amount of resources simply to realize that they are under attack. After they begin to process the message, it is too late; often the attack has already done its damage.

This is where a security gateway is required. The security gateway proxies the backend service and processes the XML or JSON message beforehand, barring malicious or badly written messages from entering the system.

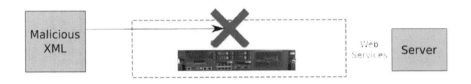

Figure 3-13 Threat protection

XML and JSON parsers intelligently determine when there is something wrong without compromising performance and prevent such data from reaching the software-based parsers in the application servers behind it. For example, it can check the length of tag names, complex nesting, and more – common attacks that are easily created to drive the consumption of software parsers. DataPower is able to detect these conditions with minimal overhead, saving your application server from using CPU cycles.

XML/JSON Schema Validation

Schema validation ensures that incoming messages conform to a known specification. The best way to detect bad content is to validate that the message adheres to the agreed upon message format. This does add additional development time to create these schema artifacts, but it is definitely worth the effort, not only will you reduce the number of threats but it will also aid in troubleshooting. You don't want to spend hours digging through code only to find out that the request should contain an integer instead of a string.

Unfortunately, in too many cases, schema validation on software-based application servers is disabled, because of the simple fact that performing schema validation is an expensive operation in terms of latency and processing power. DataPower provides the capability to do lightning-fast schema validation with minimal latency, using our XML/JSON parser that can quickly validate schemas. This means that there is no excuse not to perform schema validation on inbound request and response messages. Furthermore, you're making the most efficient use of resources by rejecting malformed requests before they ever reach the application server, saving important application server CPU cycles and helping avoid any security exposures.

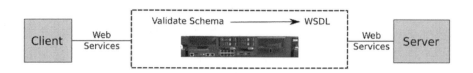

Figure 3-14 Schema Validation

DataPower deployment as a security gateway is common for both DMZ and Trusted zone scenarios. Another common scenario usage is an Enterprise Service Bus (ESB) gateway. You can combine DataPower integration capabilities with other integration solutions, such as IBM Integration Bus (IIB) to meet almost any integration requirement in a highly secure and optimized manner! DataPower provides high-speed integration and security, while IIB provides advanced integration, supporting distributed transactions, and long-running transactions.

The section below discusses the most common integration gateway scenarios.

Integration Gateway/ESB

The Integration gateway or ESB pattern has been described in many books and papers. It is an architectural style, a way of designing intermediary computer systems to process and route data to appropriate backend systems or endpoints in an efficient and secure manner. This pattern is all about service connectivity; instead of clients and servers, we talk of service consumers and service providers.

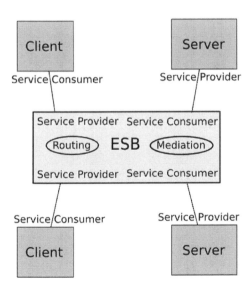

Figure 3-15 DataPower as integration gateway

Two fundamental concepts underlie the ESB style: routing and mediation. Routing in an ESB is much like network routing in concept; a service consumer connects to the bus, and the infrastructure decides on the route to the appropriate service provider. Of course, because the ESB is acting as a service provider to that consumer, it can transparently route the request to any real provider of the service that it wants. It could also respond to the consumer itself, without ever contacting a service provider; it can even contact a number of service providers, aggregate the results, and return them as a single response to the service consumer.

Mediation is a slightly more advanced concept that comes into play when service consumers and service providers do not match, when they either do not speak the same wire format, data format, schema, or any other kind of difference. Mediation bridges the differences by transforming data formats, converting transport layers, remapping data structures, and repurposing existing services such that they can fulfill others.

Finally, as an ESB performs its mediation and routing of service requests from consumers to providers and back, it by design adds more value in the form of security enforcement, service-level management and monitoring. Implementations of routing and mediation are configured, often using processing policies created from out of the box processing actions, to determine appropriate service providers. Where the device shines is in the implementation of the added value features. Performing security enforcement, token transformation, service-level management and monitoring are the bread-and-butter of the appliance, as will become apparent throughout the later chapters of this book. The next section explores the detailed ESB use cases and the role that DataPower plays in them.

Multiple Protocols

One of the core advantages of DataPower is its capability to communicate with many different technologies. Its protocol support covers a number of currently popular transport protocols, including HTTP/HTTPS, FTP/FTPS, WebSphere MQ, NFS, IMS, WebSphere JMS, and Tibco EMS.

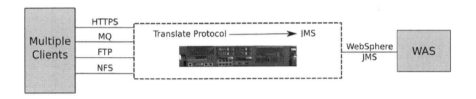

Figure 3-16 Protocol Transformation

HTTP and HTTPS are, of course, used for the most-often discussed architectures, REST and Web services. But they are also used for many other forms of communication. Sometimes integration of "traditional" Web applications, designed not for remote system use but for human interaction, is done over HTTP, with the system or bus pretending to be a human user.

FTP support is important. There are many "legacy" systems in existence whose main form of communication is files. That is, they accept input files that are put on a file system, and they produce as output other files that are put back onto the file system. To communicate with these systems, we must have a way of processing data from that remote file system; with FTP support, this becomes trivial, because almost every IP-connected system can easily be configured to communicate via FTP! However simply supporting the protocol is not enough; we must be able to support it securely, such that the administrators and owners of these legacy systems are happy allowing us to access them. Thus the DataPower implementation of FTP allows for full AAA processing and for configuration of mutually authenticated SSL over both the control and data channels as required.

Likewise, Network File System (NFS) support is key to integrating with systems that are not quite "up to date" enough to support Web services. Large shared Network Attached Storage (NAS) devices are becoming common in the enterprise and provide a shared platform over which data can be exchanged; DataPower is able to poll and process files from these NAS arrays using NFS and write files to them in response.

Finally, we cannot completely talk about integration without mentioning the messaging protocols; WebSphere MQ, WebSphere JMS, and Tibco EMS. Ever since the advent of the IBM Message Queuing protocol, asynchronous queuing has been hugely popular for two reasons. The first is that it provides an asynchronous method of submitting data for processing; that is, you write a message to a queue, and something else will deal with it in its own time. This is a great way of processing large loads at peak efficiency because business systems can draw exactly enough data to process at a time and are short of data to process only if there is no actual work to do; however there is another reason that applies to WebSphere MQ, and this is that MQ client and server software support is available for an amazing array of platforms. This means that we can use MQ to communicate with everything from a Windows server to a mainframe.

Multiple Datatypes

Just as we can communicate with many different protocols, the DataPower Gateway is actually capable of processing almost any type of data. This extremely powerful functionality in conjunction with the support for different communication protocols means that DataPower is capable of performing integration that in some cases would simply not be possible in any other way without writing significant amounts of application code—so much in fact that it would probably be simpler to re-write the backend systems! That is the value proposition: Really difficult integration work can be completed more easily using configuration on DataPower.

In addition, it is important not to forget that one of the fundamental core functions of the device is transformation of data. XSLT allows for structured and controlled transformations and translations of formats that have absolutely nothing in common with each other except for the fact that they are both expressed in XML. Similarly, JSON is used in many application services similarly to XML. JavaScript and XQuery with JSONiq extension allow you to enrich and transform JSON messages.

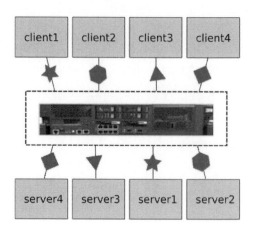

Figure 3-17 Data integration

This ability to perform many transformations is important when dealing with real-life use cases. For example, when a system provides a service, and other systems want to use that service, there is no guarantee that those other systems will be compatible. A typical enterprise might have any number of different clients all performing the same kind of processing, and all doing it with their own definition of what that processing means. Each client and each server may have its own schema and its own understanding of how to process the data, and therefore, the service provider must understand and implement all of them.

Outside of the enterprise there are also many situations in which people do similar things in a similar way, but none of the ways they do things can interoperate with each other. If you look at any given industry, it is highly likely that they will have common industry concepts that anyone performing that kind of business must be able to understand; otherwise, they would be out of business. The more established industries have, over time, defined common standards that everyone adheres to in order to be able to interoperate and communicate. However even those standards are often open to interpretation, or expanded on for commercial advantage, or worse yet competing standards arrive and need to be translated between!

Using DataPower, it is possible to process the data for all these scenarios. But what do you do with it once you have it? A useful pattern is to create what is loosely known as a "defacto schema" (sometimes also called the "golden schema"). This is a concept where you take all the common points of data and wrap them up into a single definition and representation of that data.

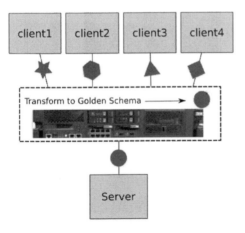

Figure 3-18 Golden schema

This is hard work, and DataPower will not magically come up with the schema for you! However DataPower provides the frontend to enable mapping of all the disparate data types and formats into this "defacto schema" so that your backend applications can work with this single, unified understanding. This leads to a far simpler development process for new applications and with time can be used to provide back to the clients (be they internal clients or industry-wide) that such-and-such a definition might be useful because it truly represents the needs of the industry.

Routing

DataPower is more than capable of handling multiple datatypes and mediating between applications. Service routing entails taking a request from a service consumer and passing it on to a service provider that will be able to fulfill that request. DataPower can route messages in a myriad of different ways, and even contains an out-of-the-box dynamic "routing" action that can be freely used in a Processing Policy. But what if, rather than simply passing through a request and passing back a response, while potentially transforming the data structure and changing the protocols, we were to take that request and provide a response by building up a number of requests to several services? Would that make DataPower the service provider or just another intermediary? This concept of brokering multiple services into a single combined composite service is known as a scatter/gather architectural pattern.

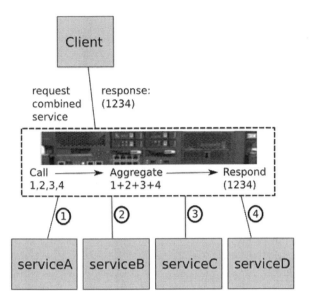

Figure 3-19 Scatter/gather pattern

The specific pattern is simple; it shows the calling of multiple services in parallel and aggregating the responses. DataPower implements this use case out of the box using the Results action, which allows you to specify the list of endpoints that the message is sent; there is an implicit synchronization point, which waits for all the responses and provides them in DataPower context variables for "aggregation" using XSLT or GatewayScript.

Governance & Management

Governance is quite often the "elephant in the room" – everybody knows it needs to be done, but people are reluctant to speak out and make it a priority. When you build your services with a governance-first attitude, you put yourself in a solid position for future growth and are better equipped to handle significant changes within your infrastructure. Just think of when you're asked to perform a firmware upgrade on DataPower, the first planning step is to understand all your service consumers and providers – without proper governance, this would be a very difficult! Implementing governance may seem relatively simple at first, but is, in fact, multi-faceted and has a lot of detail and complexity hidden within, making it as powerful and compelling problem.

The simplest form of service management is to have a central repository of service information, artifacts such as WSDL/JSON schema files, where you would track each service lifecycle, endpoints, and any other metadata about a service. DataPower integrates with WebSphere Service Registry and Repository (WSRR) to fetch service interfaces at design-time and dynamic data at runtime, such as the service provider endpoint for dynamic routing.

More advanced service management involves establishing service level agreements (SLA) for different consumers. For example different consumers of services may require different levels of service. For instance, if Client A is paying less for a service and Client B is paying more, and there is some kind of a problem that not all requests can be serviced, it seems that Client B, who is paying more for the service, should be given priority over Client A. Of course, Client A would have known up front when choosing the less expensive package that in the event of issues, other clients paying for more expensive packages would be prioritized over him.

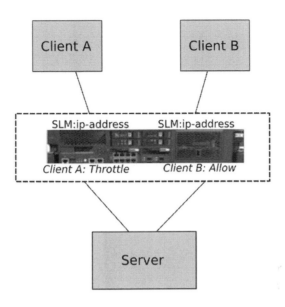

Figure 3-20 SLM Enforcement

How would we implement this on DataPower? Well, DataPower provides a facility called Service Level Monitoring (SLM). In short, the SLM capability allows for a policy-driven approach to decide which priority requests are treated. It can throttle or even deny requests that meet certain preset boundaries and conditions. This is used to enforce policies such as that described previously with different clients paying different fees for the same service but with different Service Level Agreements (SLA).

For example, if you have two backend servers that are capable of providing the service: Slow Server and Fast Server. DataPower can implement SLM based on the IP address of the client (although this could, of course, be based on any of a vast selection of transactional metadata), and this time uses that information to direct requests from Client A to Slow Server and Client B to Fast Server, thus ensuring that Client B gets a better service.

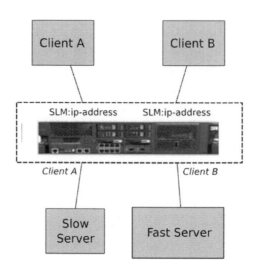

Figure 3-21 Priority-based routing

The SLM functionality can also be used to protect backend application servers from spikes in traffic. Where the capacity of a server or group of servers is known, it is possible to utilize SLM as a traffic management point where advanced traffic shaping and throttling occurs and requests are queued on the network or in the device up to a limit or until the application server is capable of processing it, or even simply rejected by configuration for specific clients until the traffic situation resolves itself.

DataPower can also integrate with WSRR for SLM policy enforcement. WSRR provide a policy authoring point to define SLM policies using a common vocabulary and then push them to DataPower for runtime enforcement – allowing you to separate the definition and enforcement of SLM policies and provide business owners with the ability to change SLAs based on business requirements without making configuration changes on DataPower.

Legacy Integration

Another important DataPower deployment topology is that of enabling legacy applications to work with modern services. Legacy applications such as CICS and IMS, usually running on mainframe computers that have been doing their jobs steadily and well for many years, are not significantly different in concept to our modern application servers. They are often designed in a similar idiom to modern form-based Web applications; the user types data into a number of fields, clicks the submit button, and the application processes the input and returns a response. However there are a number of challenges with modernizing these applications.

First of all and most important is the fact that, because these applications have been stable and running for many years, it is very hard in most environments to get a change made to the application. It is possible for implementation of changes to take months or even years! In some cases it is even all but impossible, because the source code to the applications has been lost over the years. Secondly, the applications often use older formats for data and requests, which are not well supported in the age of the Web browser or app. And finally, the applications are often not capable of communicating via the modern protocols currently in use.

DataPower is a wonderful solution to all these issues. Its support for protocol bridging and data transformation mean that it is possible to configure and front these "legacy" applications with a minimum of overhead, and significantly less effort than would be required with an application coding effort. Moreover it is usually possible to perform this integration without requiring any changes on the mainframe—often turning an impossible project into a realistic one.

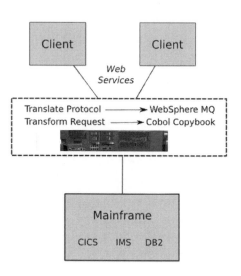

Figure 3-22 DataPower and IMS

In addition, there are extra benefits to consider. First, the legacy applications might not have data secured at a granular level of access control. When these applications were written, it was common practice to secure at the level of application access; that is, to provide an identity for a remote application after authentication, had access to do whatever it needed to the data. By leveraging DataPower's powerful AAA functionality, we can add more fine-grained security around this data.

Second, DataPower is a high-performance appliance. By offloading security and integration tasks, and additional pre-processing wherever possible, it is highly likely that less CPU (measured in MIPS) will be required on the mainframe applications. This may even lead to a reduction in cost for running those applications for some customers!

Summary

Choosing how to use DataPower is a complex decision process, because there are so many possible ways to do it, and so many places in your infrastructure where it is just a perfect fit to do the job! This chapter presented some common use cases and some ways of deploying the appliance that are known to have worked for other customers and will likely work well for you.

Appendix A: DataPower Naming Conventions

This appendix is designed to give some insight into the process of naming DataPower configuration objects, as well as providing some example names that follow the guidelines. Though every enterprise will have its own internal naming conventions that must be taken into account during a DataPower implementation, it is almost guaranteed that those conventions will not extend to the specificity needed by the multitude of internal DataPower objects.

Developers and administrators also have their own preferences for case, concatenation, and abbreviation. Feel free to impose those preferences on these guidelines. This text uses CamelCase; however, hyphenated (-) names, underscored (_) names, and ALL_CAPS names are also acceptable (syntactically) as DataPower object names. Use your favorite. Even if you don't agree with these conventions, it's important to follow standard naming rules in your DataPower configurations for reusability and for collaboration.

Note that the examples in this book are just that, examples. As such, they do not always follow these naming guidelines; they are designed more for demonstration purposes than for true configuration creation.

General Guidelines

These guidelines are designed for maximum reusability, from both configuration management and environment promotion perspectives. Though ideal conditions may dictate that each logical environment (development, testing, preproduction, and production) have its own DataPower device, this is sometimes not the case in real-world situations. Usually, there is a load-balanced group of two or more devices in production, hopefully with an exact replica in pre-production and/or disaster recovery. Occasionally, all other environments are shared on a single device. This setup is definitely not recommended and introduces additional complexity for environment promotion.

Although this is essentially a configuration management issue, it has an effect on naming conventions as well. Objects should be able to be moved from domain to domain (and device to device) with minimal manual modifications, as described in Chapter 15, "Build and Deploy Techniques." Ideally, this will be a completely automated process, and the more changes that have to be made (to an XML config file, CLI script, or XML Management request), the more complicated and error-prone the process becomes. So, when in doubt, design for clarity and reusability.

The other important principle to keep in mind is functional explanation. In a clear but concise manner, an object's name should represent the functional logic of the configuration held within. It should be instantly recognizable by both you and any of your colleagues, and when seen in context with its object type, it should represent the task it performs.

Name Changes

After an object has been created with a given name, that name cannot be easily modified. As such, make sure you get the name right the first time and verify that your name will represent the object in every environment to which it can potentially be deployed.

Names

The suggested naming conventions are grouped by object or object category. Each contains the naming scheme, at least one example, and some explicative reasoning for why the naming choice has been made.

Device

There are few places where devices actually require names (other than their several TCP/IP hostnames for connectivity). They usually require a name when used as an identifier to external servers, such as syslog daemons, or as a notice on the login page. The audience for these names will sometimes be different than the DataPower development audience and, thus, may be designated by personnel in other departments (typically, networking or security). These names must differentiate between multiple devices in a given environment, sometimes even between this and other non-appliance servers and routers, and may need to contain hints about physical location. As such, this is one of the least standardized names. We strongly suggest you name all of your devices by navigating to *Administration→Device→System Settings* in the left-side menu and choosing a System Identifier; here are a few examples:

- XmlGwDMZ01

- XG45Dev03

- DPProd17

- XI52TucsonStaging02

Application Domain

The name of an application domain depends quite a bit on your designated architecture, from device management, project management, and environment promotion perspectives. Domains can be created for a development team, a project team, or even for a single user (in a development setting). Single user and other sandbox domain names are less important than those that might travel between appliances, but their names should still be descriptive. For those that will be promoted between environments, the name should contain the development group or project name. If DataPower appliances are deployed in multiple corporate security zones, each with its own version of a domain, then the name should also reflect its eventual destination, even if all development is done on a single internal device. Here are a few options:

- HRServices

- AccountServicesDMZ

- AccountServicesInternal

- NextGenInfrastructure

- JoeSmith

- MainframeServices

TIP—Versioning Domain Names

Many DataPower users will include version identifiers in domain names. This can help to avoid ending up with domain names like "NewerNextGenInfrastructure".

Service

A service name should give some indication of what is represented by the configuration. In a Web Service Proxy (WSP), this generally means the service it protects; however, WSPs can also contain multiple WSDLs, each referencing a related service with unique features. In these cases, the name should be more generic, representing the full cluster of categorized services. In these cases, when built upon one or more Web services, the name will often be followed by "Service" or "Services." For services without an existing Web service name, you should consider the full path of a message that might be flowing through this service: it will enter the device in a particular format on a given protocol, be processed in some fashion, and be delivered to a backend server in (perhaps) another format or protocol. Your name should reflect the full progression, especially if there will be a format, protocol, or message transformation involved. Here are some examples:

- ImagingService/ImagingServices

- MapHTTPToMQ

- ConvertEDIToXML
- BillingServices
- BridgeMQToEMS

What these names should not do is contain the name of the environment in which the service resides. Even if this is a development environment, naming your Web Service Proxy ImagingServiceDev will only cause problems when you go to promote this environment to QA. You should always look for this balance between generality and descriptiveness; keep it general enough to move between domains and environments, while still providing clues to the processing contained therein. Services are also always grouped by type when displayed by the administrative tools, so there's no need to distinguish between ImagingServiceMPGW, ImagingServiceXMLFW, and ImagingServiceWSP—just call it ImagingService.

Service Types

These service naming criteria apply to all major service types, including XML Firewall, Multiprotocol Gateway, Web Service Proxy, Web Application Firewall, XSL Proxy, and the lesser-known services available from the left-side menus.

Processing Policy

A processing policy is tied closely to the service in which it resides, as each service can contain only one policy. As such, a processing policy usually has the same name as its service, minus any reference to the protocols being invoked. A policy can be used by multiple services, perhaps of different types with different protocols; this name should focus entirely on the processing taking place within and ignore the type of service or the protocols for frontend and backend connections. ConvertEDIToXML is still a valid name because it focuses on the message format rather than the protocol; MapHTTPToMQ would be significantly less useful. In these cases, focus on the actions within: AddMQHeaders or RouteToMQBackend would be more appropriate. Note that policies within a Web Service Proxy are not named by the user and are not reusable in other services.

Processing Rule

A processing rule name should be much more specific than a processing policy, as a policy can contain multiple rules that perform different tasks. These objects are named automatically according to the processing policy if a name is not manually defined, but this simply appends a number to the policy name, such as PolicyName_rule_0. For more specificity and potential reuse, a rule should be named according to its processing logic. More importantly, the name should distinguish between different rules within the same policy; you should be able to determine their functional differences without inspecting the actions contained therein. A rule named StripAttachments is completely distinguishable from another named VirusCheckAttachments. If the rule performs more than one major function, feel free to concatenate the important ones. Focusing on the main purpose of a processing rule will result in names such as the following:

- ProcessAttachments
- StripAttachments

- SignEncrypt

- TransformSignEncrypt

If you are not interested in taking advantage of the reusability of these rules, and they will appear only in the processing policy in which they've been defined, you may want to include the processing policy name as a prefix. In this case, AttachmentServiceProcessAttachments and AttachmentServiceStripAttachments could be separate rules in the AttachmentService processing policy.

Match Rule

Each processing rule begins with a match action that defines which incoming messages will be executed by that rule. Match rules are reusable, so they should be named according to their matching criteria so that they may be used appropriately and easily. These criteria can vary widely because matching can take place on headers, URLs, error codes, and even message content. The following could all be useful matching rule names:

- MatchAll

- MatchSAMLAssertion

- MatchBackendConnectionError

- MatchBinarySecurityToken

Front Side Handlers

Each MPGW or WSP service can have multiple Front Side Handlers, listening for requests on various protocols. These should be named according to the service to which they are attached and should include the protocol. For Web Service Proxies, this may reference a group of services. Examples are as follows:

- ImagingServiceMQ

- HRServicesHttps

- CreditServiceFTP

WARNING—Including Port Numbers in Names

HTTP and HTTPS listener names can include a port, but you should only do so if this port will not be modified between environments. The port addition is especially useful when looking at a list of services or at a list of FSH within a service—the port is not shown unless you open the FSH object itself, so including the number (in an accurate and consistent manner) can save a step. However, keep in mind that these names can't be easily changed. If the HRServicesHttps443 Front Side Handler might be copied to another domain and modified to listen on 8443, then don't include the port number in the name!

XML Manager

Although many services can use the default XML Manager, simple changes often need to be made, such as the addition of a Load Balancer Group, modification of parser behavior, or definition of a caching policy. In these cases, you should always create a new XML Manager (don't modify the default one!) and name it after the modifications. This would result in names similar to the following:

- ParseRestrictions

- CacheDocuments

- BackendLoadBalancer

If you simply modify the default XML Manager, there is the potential to unwittingly impose those modifications on a new service that you (or someone else in the same domain) create in the future. That object is also less likely to be noticed and successfully imported when moving objects between domains or devices.

User Agent

In the same fashion that an XML Manager controls parsing and caching behavior for the incoming message, a user agent controls connection behavior between DataPower and any backend servers. Any user agent requirements should be created in a new object (don't modify the default one!) and should be named after the modifications contained therein. This results in names similar to the following:

- InjectSOAPActions

- FTPCredentials

- ProxyServerConfig

- HTTP10Policy

AAA Policy

Within a processing rule, a AAA policy can provide access control for inbound messages. These are highly reusable, as the accepted input credentials, authentication/authorization methodologies, and backend token formats are likely to be similar for various services. If the policy is being used for token exchange, its name should reflect the input and output token formats. BasicAuthToSAML and UsernameTokenToLTPA would be useful in this case. If the policy is simply authenticating and authorizing without producing a backend token, then you should name the policy based on the servers being used for each. LDAPAuth and TAMAuAz are both distinctive and descriptive.

Certificate

Certificate objects on the DataPower appliance encapsulate certificate files for abstraction purposes. This allows the actual file to have a name descriptive of the environment for which it is used, while keeping the object name generic enough to be promoted to a new environment without a need for modification. The object name should describe its place in the logical architecture rather than referencing a specific hostname. A certificate imported from an LDAP server for LDAPS interaction should be called LDAPServer, rather than DevLDAP. WASBackend could be another internal server, while InternalHRClient could represent a certificate used for mutual authentication to an internal HR application. XYCorpServices could represent the server certificate delivered by services.xyco.com; it is non-representative of an application environment, but still self-explanatory.

Key

Key objects are generally paired to certificate objects that will be used on the device for encryption by a partner, SSL server identification, or digital signature creation. As such, the names of objects referencing key files should be tied very closely to the names of the objects referencing the certificate files with which they are paired.

Identification Credential

An Identification Credential represents the pairing of a key object to a certificate object. They are then used for SSL server identification and other document encryption and decryption tasks. ID credentials should be named the same as the certificate they contain so that it is obvious which key pair they are referencing.

Validation Credential

A validation credential is used for verifying incoming certificates used for SSL mutual authentication and other cryptographic tasks. Because this object can contain multiple certificates, it is often impossible to reference them all in the object name. Focus on the group of certificate owners that need to be validated or the type of certificates expected. Sample names can be similar to the following:

- PublicCerts

- InternalCARoot

- DotNetWAS

- ApprovedExternalClients

Crypto Profile

A crypto profile provides a method for combining cryptographic objects for use in an SSL connection. The included objects depend on whether the appliance is acting as a server (backend) or a client (frontend) and whether Mutual Authentication is necessary. These two criteria, as well as an indication of the service itself, should be included in the crypto profile name. Use the service name, followed by the type of SSL (client or server) then followed by an optional MA for mutual authentication. This results in sample names such as the following:

- InternalServicesServer

- BackendServicesClient

- HRServicesServerMA

SSL Proxy Profile

A SSL proxy profile consists of either one or two Crypto Profile objects, tying those objects to a particular service as either a reverse (server) SSL connection, a forward (client) SSL connection, or a two-way (both server and client) connection. For forward or reverse, the object should have the exact same name as the crypto profiles they reference. For two-way SSL, remove the reference to Client or Server and replace it with the phrase TwoWay. This results in a name such as HRServicesTwoWayMA.

Queuing Technologies

The general category of queuing technologies encompasses several different DataPower objects. The same naming guidelines apply to each, as they all require an initial configuration of the connection to the management server—that object is then referenced in the actual connection URL or Front Side Handler. These objects include the MQ Queue

Manager, Tibco EMS server, and WebSphereJMS; non-messaging-server interface objects such as IMS Connect and SQL Data Source would have similar naming conventions. Names for these objects should reference the logical architecture rather than their physical location or application environment. Avoid hostnames, references to development, QA, production, and datacenter names. If the queuing server will act as a bridge between two architectural zones, reference them both. There is no need to reference the protocol itself, as these objects are each in their own lists, categorized by object. Examples are as follows:

- DMZInternet

- DMZIntranet

- InternalWASCluster

- HRMainframeApp

Log Target

Log targets represent a subscription to a set of log events that will be designated to be sent to a specific target over any one of a number of protocols. A log target name should represent the type and priority of the events to which it is subscribed, as well as the target of those events. If there are filters on the events, the object or event being filtered should be included as well. Examples can include

- EmergencyToSNMP

- AlertToSMTP

- CertMonitorToAppSyslog

- AAAToSecuritySyslog

- HRServicesProxyErrorToFTP

Transforms (XSLT or GatewayScript)

There are many cases in which files need to be uploaded to the device (or referenced from a remote location). There may be existing corporate naming conventions for files containing code and in that case those should be used rather than our suggestions. For files that will be used in Transform actions, names should represent the logic inherent within. Here are some examples (substitute a .js extension for GatewayScript):

- CheckAttachment.xsl

- StripWSSecurity.xsl

- AuthorizeLDAPGroups.xsl

Filters (XSLT)

Filter files are also XSLT transformations and should also be named by logic. However, because these will be used in a Filter action, that should be appended to the end of the filename. An example of a filter that checks for negative inputs would be SQLInjectionFilter.xsl, while one that checks for valid inputs would be ValidFormContentsFilter.xsl.

Configuration Files (XML)

Additional XML files used for configurations, user data, and other on-board uses should be named for the data contained within. Example names could be UserRegistry.xml, RoutingTable.xml, or AAAForHR.xml.

Summary

There are many objects that can be configured on the DataPower appliance, including some that are not explicitly referenced in this chapter. As long as you keep in mind the two guiding principles for name creation—descriptiveness and reusability/portability—you should be able to extend the concepts laid out here to fit any other object on the device. The names will then become common sense, and you can create objects named HRServicesDevelopers (for a UserGroup), PerMappedCredential (for a SLM Credential Class), and EncryptSocSecNbr (for a Document Crypto Map). Following these guidelines will assist with collaboration, reuse, and easy documentation among development groups. Use them to finalize your own naming conventions that will be used and enforced in your environment.

Appendix B: Deployment Checklist

DataPower is well known for its ease of configuration. Those quick configuration exercises are great for demos and quick one-off tests, but when it comes to rolling out anything into production, great care must be taken. Often, the best-laid deployment plans go awry due to haste, lack of planning, or miscommunication. It takes only one missed step during deployment to thwart the careful planning and hard work of entire teams of architects, developers, and testers. Backing out a botched deploy isn't pleasant. The deployment process is something that is best done quickly and efficiently, particularly because, in some cases, systems are down or applications are unavailable during deployment. This appendix provides a checklist of things to think about before the actual process starts. This can (and should) be augmented with many of the other environment-specific tips and techniques found in the text of this book.

Testing

T1. Have unit, integrated, performance, functional, negative, and acceptance testing been completed satisfactorily? Just because DataPower is an appliance does not mean that testing should not be done. Testing against this platform using the same tools and methodologies you test your transactional backend systems with is important. What are the detailed, reproducible, and carefully reviewed results of these tests? (Yes, those things are all important.)

T2. Can all Service Level Agreements (SLA), such as response time under a peak-simulated load, be met, including the overhead of authentication/authorization if they are required? Is this also the case when failover occurs during reasonable failure scenarios? If DataPower is configured for high availability and some of the dependent components (such as LDAP directories) are not, then you do not have high availability. The system has a single point of failure (SPOF) and can be brought down by the failure of a single component.

T3. Has failover been verified by "disconnecting" components to simulate runtime failures? Do any single points of failure exist and has the "Rule of Threes" (if it takes two of something to handle peak load, then you need three in case one fails) been taken into account? Has failover testing been done while load testing is under way to test the behavior under duress? Remember, high availability is a system-wide thing, and should also be tested (no matter how painful it is to pull that plug).

T4. Were the final pre-production or staging tests done in an environment identical to production? (Or if not, are the deltas and associated risks well documented?)

T5. Have members of other infrastructure areas (network, database, and operating system) been involved in testing and have they made tuning changes to accommodate the new deployment?

T6. Have all functional and nonfunctional requirements been signed off?

T7. Have the users been prepared and trained? Will they have the opportunity to use the prior version for some period of time?

Security

S1. Have security requirements been carefully defined and the system implementation evaluated against those requirements? Has a security expert reviewed the system design and implementation? Have all system components outside of DataPower been hardened? Has the network topology been reviewed for possible sensitive traffic "in the clear"?

S2. Has the DataPower system certificate been replaced with a self-signed certificate or certificate from a legitimate Certificate Authority? Instructions for doing this are in the WebGUI Guide.

S3. Has any form of ethical hacking been done, at a minimum turning some of the more "creative" employees loose on the system as a challenge?

S4. Have expiration dates been checked and documented on all certificates and passwords? Is there a clear plan for updating these when needed? Is monitoring in place to alert administrators when they near expiration? (Don't depend on someone checking the logs on a regular basis!)

S5. Has it been verified that all identities used for connecting to backend resources, such as databases, are valid for the new environment being deployed to and have the correct privileges assigned to them?

S6. Have access violations been captured in a Log Target and rolled off the device to a persistent location? Tracking these may help to identify attempts to compromise the system.

S7. Has administrative access to the device been limited to a well-defined group of users connecting on a management network? Make sure everyone isn't sharing a single admin account, particularly not the "admin" userid.

S8. Have password policies been established to ensure they meet internal security policies and are changed periodically?

Environment

E1. Will all necessary userids/passwords for DataPower and other components be available for the deployment? It is a common theme to get to the deployment date and not have correct privileges to deploy some component into the target environment—for example, not having the admin password for a firewall to allow traffic to pass from DataPower to the backend over the configured port(s).

E2. Has it been verified that all infrastructure components are fully operational, with no errors occurring in the logs? As part of "sanity checking," all logs should be checked for DataPower and other system components to ensure there are no early warning signs of production failure when the go switch is flipped.

E3. Is all necessary information (for example, server names and port numbers) available for resources such as databases or legacy systems? Has connectivity to these resources from the target environment been verified?

E4. Have all network traffic routes through firewalls, switches, and routers been verified? Are documents showing the topology, firewall rules, and so on up to date and available for troubleshooting?

E5. Are Log Targets being used to capture critical log events and are they being moved off the device to persistent locations?

E6. Is there plenty of space on persistent volumes used for logging? Has capacity planning been done for all system components?

E7. Has configuration data for both pre-deploy and post-deploy been checked into change management?

E8. Has it been verified that there is appropriate monitoring and that alerts go to the appropriate places?

E9. Are all commercial software infrastructure components at the appropriate version/fixpack levels? Are all vendor prerequisites in place?

E10. Have all "test harnesses" or test-only configurations and stubs been removed?

E11. Have configurations for logging been turned down to production levels? You don't want to go live with logging set at the debug level!

E12. Have all probes been disabled in all domains in all devices? Having these enabled can impact performance as well as the security of sensitive production data.

Deployment Process

D1. Have all team member responsibilities and their status for the deployment date been verified?

D2. Is there a well-defined reproducible deployment process? There should be a clear document describing the process. Is the deployment process automated? If not, see Chapter 15, "Build and Deploy Techniques."

D3. Have deployment scripts (where used) been verified prior to deployment in production-like environments? It is important to test and exercise these scripts as part of moving the configuration through the various stages of testing—unit, integration, performance, QA, failover, system, preproduction—to ensure that the deployment scripts themselves work and will not fail at the critical hour. Deployment should be a fast and boring job!

D4. Has the build been verified to include all components at the correct version level if you are building your domains in a granular fashion (for example, creating a new domain and importing at the services level or below in the object hierarchy from version control)?

D5. Have all team members reviewed the rollout plan (downtime, rolling servers, and so on)?

D6. Have arrangements been made to have representatives of various infrastructure areas such as network, operating system, legacy system, and database admins available in case there are problems? Have those persons been briefed on how the new DataPower applications interact with their areas, so they can anticipate problems or react more quickly should they occur?

D7. Will the DataPower application architect and key developers be available for troubleshooting in case there are problems?

D8. Are initialization scripts—such as those to "prime" the application's listeners and caches after it has been deployed, or precompile stylesheets, or test for successful response codes from applications—in place and tested?

D9. Is there a test for success for the production deployment and a backout plan in case of problems? Has the backout plan been tested? This is a critical step that is often forgotten due to teams focusing on the "happy path."

D10. Are all team members in agreement that the deployment should proceed? Ask one more time to "speak now or forever hold your peace."

D11. Have separate provisions been made to deploy artifacts that are not exported by DataPower, such as keys and certificates and user account passwords?

Administration

A1. Are all DataPower administrative IDs/roles in place on the device or for RBM?

A2. Is there a process for log file review and archival?

A3. Have all operational procedures (such as backup, disaster recovery) been tested?

A4. Are all product licenses and support agreements up to date for the intended environment?

A5. Has the help desk received proper training and documentation on the new deployment? Is there a well-defined process for fixing production problems? This includes well-defined phone numbers, pager access numbers, call lists, and escalation procedures.

A6. Have the IBM Customer Account information and contact procedures been supplied to the help desk should they need to contact IBM DataPower Support?

A7. Is a system monitoring process in place? How will the system be monitored to ensure that it is running? How will its logs and errors be monitored to capture potential problems before they become serious?

A8. Does the monitoring process include monitoring load and other resource usage? Is that information being used to predict future load and system needs? Have you taken into account load spikes that might be based on calendar events or perhaps special marketing events?

We've tried to pick out the "usual suspects" in terms of things to look out for as deployment to production nears. We're sure there are others that have occurred to you as you read this. This list should be customized for your own environment and requirements. It's meant to be just a start, but hopefully a good one!

Appendix C: DataPower Evolution

Just like any hardware or software product, DataPower has evolved over time and will continue to advance to meet the changing needs of its customers and the evolving IT industry. This appendix takes a brief look at the past, present, and future of DataPower and its product line. We discuss its history (both corporate and technical) to demonstrate how the DataPower product line has grown with the market for such devices. We discuss specific updates in both hardware and firmware, and the progression of the appliance model as applied to industry verticals.

DataPower History

DataPower was originally formed by a group of MIT alumni with an interest in using hardware appliances to solve problems that were traditionally approached with a focus on software solutions. In the process, they created a new market for network devices. IBM acquired DataPower in October 2005. Through it all, DataPower's technical solutions have continued to evolve with the changing of the IT landscape.

Performance

DataPower appeared in 1999 as a response to the advent and increasing popularity of XML as a message format. Though much more human-readable and self-descriptive than previously defined formats such as EDI, CSV, and Cobol Copybooks, XML is also verbose, resulting in a large memory and CPU footprint when parsed or transformed. Existing software parsers based solely on Document Object Model (DOM) or Simple API for XML (SAX) methodologies were slow and had significant drawbacks; transformation and schema validation engines were even less efficient. DataPower overcame these performance implications using a new, patented parser technology to create a secure, efficient platform for XML processing and transformation. When combined with specialized hardware for execution of these expensive operations, the eventual result of these efforts was the DataPower XA35 XML Acceleration appliance.

Security

XML parsing performance improvements made DataPower appliances an invaluable addition to many IT architectures requiring accelerated rendering of XML content as HTML and other browser-based formats. As XML usage matured, however, it began to be used for more than just content storage; communication of XML formatted messages to business partners allowed for easy data exchange. Message structures could be defined using standard specifications (XML Schema), and data arrived in a self-descriptive format that required less in the way of tight coupling between applications and software platforms. The ability to share data, even at high speeds, came with a price; DataPower recognized that the security of this data (privacy, integrity, and access control) was paramount to the success of this new paradigm. As the initial specifications around Web services arose (SOAP and WSDL, especially), the need for related security standards became obvious. The WS-Security specifications fit the bill but were complex and difficult to implement. The DataPower XS40 Security Appliance addresses this challenge, enforcing security policies and implementing complex encryption and digital signature specifications at wire speed through a user-friendly click-to-configure GUI. With a sophisticated interface and full support for many industry-standard security protocols, the XS40 shortened time-to-market and increased confidence in application security.

Integration

Often, industry trends come full circle. Though the popularity of XML is in part a response to the complex, machine-readable data formats of yesteryear, those old formats (and the applications that rely on them) will not soon fade away. Instead, the challenge is to re-use those existing applications and make them available as services, while at the same time incorporating advanced security and performance characteristics. The DataPower XI50 Integration Appliance addresses this need through support for many protocols, including messaging technologies (WebSphere MQ, WebSphere JMS, and Tibco EMS), common mainframe interfaces such as IMS, database and file interfaces (SQL, FTP, and NFS). In addition, the XI50 can perform any-to-any message format transformation, allowing access to applications written in COBOL and other legacy languages.

DataPower Hardware

Though DataPower hardware has had several revisions in the many years since the company's founding, the truly important evolution has been in the area of firmware. The firmware contains the patented technologies used for message processing; the SSL and cryptographic hardware accelerators don't need to be updated to add additional features.

Subsequent hardware generations (9002 and 9003) were very similar to the 9001, with minor updates in certain components. Both have four Ethernet interfaces and use flash memory as an on-device store; the 9003 hardware also has dual power supplies.

The hardware model known as the 9004 generation (or machine type 9235) adds additional on-board storage, with a choice between a RAID-mirrored pair of hard drives and a user-replaceable Compact Flash drive. It also contains iSCSI support for connections to Storage Area Networks (SAN). These additions allow for significant local logging if desired; the Compact Flash support continues to provide an alternative option with no spinning media. Prior to the 9004 hardware, any hardware issues were subject to the replacement of the entire device. The 9004 model introduced user-swappable power supplies, hard drives, fans, and battery.

The 9005 generation introduced greatly expanded network, memory and disk capacity. The enhanced memory provided response caching support on the appliance. You won't ever have to worry about running out of network modules, with 4 x 1 GbE & 2 x 10 GbE adapters on the 1U appliance and 8 x 1 GbE & 2 x 10 GbE on the 2U appliance.

The new 9006 single-device model further enhanced the processing capabilities. This is all in keeping with Moore's Law—newer hardware will typically use newer, faster technologies! The 9006 appliances provide increased CPU, memory and a faster crypto acceleration card to enhance performance of transport and message processing. Furthermore, serviceability and hardware diagnostics were enhanced to aid in identifying and resolving hardware issues.

DataPower Firmware

As mentioned earlier, the true power of DataPower functionality lies within the device's firmware. This user-upgradeable firmware image contains all the features and specification support used by the device and is constantly evolving with changing IT standards.

DataPower maintains a firmware release schedule dedicated to providing maximum customer value with a manageable volume of new releases. Point releases are made available for bug fixes and other minor modifications. Each image is accompanied by release notes describing any behavior changes, documentation updates, and known issues.

Though this book is focused on recent firmware releases and includes discussion of new and evolving features, previous firmware revisions may not contain some of the functionality we have discussed. The release notes and user documentation for your firmware image should be used as the final authority on what features are available.

Similarly, DataPower is constantly adding new features, some of which may not be described within this book. As the specifications surrounding Web 2.0, cloud, mobile, Web services and other critical IT technologies evolve, so too does the DataPower firmware. As an example, some past additions have involved support for nonstandard (Microsoft and BEA)

WS-Policy implementations, enhancements to the existing Tibco EMS support, and even additional protocol support in the form of SFTP Server functionality on a Front Side Handler. Check the release notes for all the latest changes.

As standards rapidly change to meet a fluid marketplace, DataPower shields programmers from needing to update their applications. DataPower is dedicated to keeping up with these evolving standards, and firmware releases are frequent enough to support new standard levels as they become accepted within the industry.

Additional Appliances

The value of using a network device to commoditize complex processes with simple configurations has been well demonstrated by IBM's success with the DataPower product line. However, broad concepts such as security and integration are not the only arenas that can benefit from this technology. Companies in some industries can also gain a competitive edge using the appliance model for more specific challenges.

B2B Appliance

The DataPower XB60 B2B Appliance provides a high throughput secure entry point at the edge for routing data into the enterprise. Specifically geared toward protocols such as AS2 and AS3, this device leverages DataPower's core performance, security, and integration features to provide value in a B2B environment.

Core capabilities of the XB620 include trading partner profile management, a B2B transaction viewer, and end-to-end document correlation. This device provides a hardened infrastructure for protocol and message level security in DMZ deployments and a full-featured user interface for simplified B2B configuration, management, and deployment.

Virtual Appliances

Introduced in late 2012, the DataPower XG45 and XI52 virtual editions provide the physical appliance functionality in a virtual form factor. DataPower virtual edition allows you to use the same purpose-built firmware that runs on the physical appliance, providing deployment flexibility either on-premise, in PureSystems or on the cloud in SoftLayer.

You can deploy virtual appliances on commodity hardware provisioned with a supported hypervisor. You are now responsible for tuning the CPU, memory, network, and securing the physical hardware that will run the DataPower virtual machine. Configuration can be migrated seamlessly between virtual and physical appliances, so a possibly topology could use virtual appliances in development and test environments and physical appliances in staging and production.

Physical appliances provide enhanced security and performance compared to virtual appliances, which are more important in staging and production environments. You are entitled to the latest firmware release (as long as you pay your support bills!) and usage as a warm or cold standby at no-charge.

Cloud Editions

Cloud platforms are extremely important in today's IT landscape and architectures. Firmware version 7.2 expanded support to SoftLayer CloudLayer Computing Instance (CCI) and Amazon Elastic Compute Cloud (EC2). These cloud environments provide elastic on-demand capabilities so that workloads can be scaled at lower costs when circumstances demand more or less computing power. These are Infrastructure as a Service (IaaS) offerings. DataPower is also part of IBM's Bluemix Platform as a Service platform offering.

DataPower also provides a Secure Gateway service that can be used to securely connect IBM Bluemix applications to on premise applications in hybrid cloud architectures. This allows for quick connectivity without having to make firewall changes while still allowing controlled access. It also provides for load balancing and fault tolerance in these scenarios.

Summary

This appendix and this book focused on various aspects of the DataPower Gateway Appliances, from hardware to firmware to features. You've learned how these devices are purpose-built to solve IT problems and how you can configure them to perform valuable, reusable tasks in a variety of different use cases. We hope you have gained enough insight to use these appliances, introduce them into your architectures, and love them as much as we do. Good luck!

Appendix D: Acronyms Glossary

AAA   Authentication, Authorization, Auditing

ACL   Access Control List

AJAX   Asynchronous JavaScript and XML

ARP   Address Resolution Protocol

BST   Binary Security Token

CA   Certificate Authority

CIDR   Classless Inter-Domain Routing

CLI   Command Line Interface

CSV   Comma Separated Values

DHCP   Dynamic Host Configuration Protocol

DIME   Direct Internet Message Encapsulation

DMZ   Demilitarized Zone

DN   Distinguished Name

DNS   Domain Name System

DOM   Document Object Model

DSIG   Digital Signature

DTD   Data Type Definition

EDI   Electronic Data Interchange

EMS   Enhanced Messaging Service or Enterprise Messaging Service

ESB   Enterprise Service Bus

FFD   Flat File Descriptor

FTP   File Transfer Protocol

FTPS   File Transfer Protocol over Secure Socket Layer

HMAC   Hash Message Authentication Code

HSM   Hardware Storage Module

HTTP   Hypertext Transfer Protocol

HTTPS Hypertext Transfer Protocol over Secure Socket Layer

ICAP   Internet Content Adaptation Protocol

ICMP   Internet Control Message Protocol

IDE   Integrated Development Environment

IDS   Intrusion Detection System

IMS   Information Management System

IP   Internet Protocol

iSCSI   Internet Small Computer System Interface

Java EE Java Enterprise Edition

JDBC   Java Database Connectivity

JMS   Java Message Service

JSON   JavaScript Object Notation

JVM   Java Virtual Machine

JWE   JSON Web Encryption

JWK   JSON Web Key

JWS   JSON Web Signature

JWT   JSON Web Token

KDC   Key Distribution Center

LDAP   Lightweight Directory Access Protocol

LTPA   Lightweight Third-Party Authentication

MAC   Media Access Control

MD5   Message Digest Algorithm Number 5

MIB   Management Information Base

MIME   Multipurpose Internet Mail Extensions

MQ   IBM WebSphere MQ

MQMD   MQ Message Descriptor

MTOM   Message Transmission Optimization Mechanism

NFS   Network File System

NTP   Network Time Protocol

ODBC   Open Database Connectivity

OID   Object Identifier

PDP   Policy Decision Point

PEP   Policy Enforcement Point

PKI   Public Key Infrastructure

PCRE   Perl Compatible Regular Expression

QA   Quality Assurance

QM   Queue Manager

RAID   Redundant Array of Independent Disks

REST   Representational State Transfer

RFC   Request For Comments

RFH   MQ Rules and Formatting Header

RFH2   MQ Rules and Formatting Header 2

SAML   Security Assertion Markup Language

SAN   Storage Area Network

SAX   Simple API for XML

SCM   Source Configuration Management

SCP   Secure Copy Protocol

SFTP   Secure File Transfer Protocol

SHA-1   Secure Hash Algorithm number 1

SLA   Service Level Agreement

SLM   Service Level Monitoring or Service Level Management

SMTP   Simple Mail Transfer Protocol

SNMP   Simple Network Management Protocol

SOA   Service Oriented Architecture

SOAP   Once known as Simple Object Access Protocol, though no longer an acronym

SPNEGO Simple and Protected GSS API Negotiation Mechanism

SQL   Structured Query Language

SSH   Secure Shell

SSL   Secure Sockets Layer

TAM   Tivoli Access Manager

TCP   Transmission Control Protocol

TFIM   Tivoli Federated Identity Manager

TLS   Transport Layer Security

UDDI   Universal Description Discovery and Integration

UDP   User Datagram Protocol

UNT   Username Token

URI   Uniform Resource Identifier

URL   Uniform Resource Locator

WSDL   Web Services Description Language

WSRR   IBM WebSphere Service Registry and Repository

WAS   IBM WebSphere Application Server

WML   Wireless Markup Language

WSDM   Web Services Distributed Management

WTX   IBM WebSphere Transformation Extender

XACML   XML Access Control Markup Language

XML   Extensible Markup Language

XMLDSIG   XML Digital Signature

XMLENC   XML Encryption

XPath   XML Path Language

XSD   XML Schema Definition

XSL   Extensible Stylesheet Language

XSLT   Extensible   Stylesheet   Language   for
Transformations

Appendix E: DataPower Resources

IBM DataPower Knowledge Center:

http://www-01.ibm.com/support/knowledgecenter/SS9H2Y/welcome

Information Center:

http://www.ibm.com/software/integration/datapower/library/documentation

Internet/WWW Main Product Page:

http://www.ibm.com/datapower

DataPower GitHub:

https://github.com/ibm-datapower

Twitter:

https://twitter.com/IBMGateways

YouTube:

https://www.youtube.com/channel/UCV2_-gdea5LM58S-E3WCqew

LinkedIn:

https://www.linkedin.com/groups?home=&gid=4820454

developerWorks Discussion Forum:

https://www.ibm.com/developerworks/community/forums/html/forum?id=11111111-0000-0000-0000-000000001198

Weekly DataPower Webcast:

https://www14.software.ibm.com/webapp/iwm/web/signup.do?source=swg-wdwfw

SlideShare:

http://www.slideshare.net/ibmdatapower/

How-to find appropriate DataPower product information:

http://www-01.ibm.com/support/docview.wss?uid=swg21377654

DataPower Product Support Website:

Contains firmware, documentation, support procedure, technotes and other helpful material:

http://www.ibm.com/software/integration/datapower/support/

Redbooks:

http://www.redbooks.ibm.com/cgi-bin/searchsite.cgi?query=datapower

Software Services for WebSphere:

Ttop-notch DataPower consulting from IBM WebSphere.

http://www.ibm.com/developerworks/websphere/services/findbykeyword.html?q1=DataPower

Hermann Stamm-Wilbrandt's Blog:

Hermann is one of the brightest minds in DataPower-land, and his blog on development topics is incredibly valuable, featuring tips and techniques that can't be found elsewhere.

https://www.ibm.com/developerworks/community/blogs/HermannSW/?lang=en

WebSphere Global Community DataPower Group:

http://www.websphereusergroup.org/datapower

IBM WebSphere DataPower Support:

http://www.ibm.com/software/integration/datapower/support/

Support Flashes RSS Feed:

http://www-947.ibm.com/systems/support/myfeed/xmlfeeder.wss?feeder.requid=feeder.create_public_feed&feeder.feedtype=RSS&feeder.maxfeed=25&OC=SS9H2Y&feeder.subdefkey=swgws&feeder.channel.title=WebSphere%20DataPower%20SOA%20Appliances&feeder.channel.descr=The%20latest%20updates%20about%20WebSphere%20DataPower%20SOA%20Appliances

IBM DataPower Support Technotes:

http://www.ibm.com/search/csass/search?q=&sn=spe&lang=en&filter=collection:stgsysx,dblue,ic,pubs,devrel1&prod=U692969C82819Q63

IBM Education Assistant DataPower Modules:

http://www-01.ibm.com/support/knowledgecenter/websphere_iea/com.ibm.iea.wdatapower/plugin_coverpage.dita

WAMC Technote:

http://www-01.ibm.com/support/docview.wss?uid=swg24032265

DataPower Feature Grid:

We consider the Feature Grid to be an invaluable resource, and we are excited to provide it to you. It yields the answers to the most commonly asked questions about DataPower ("Is feature/protocol/spec X supported on my Y appliance?") We had initially included the entire table here, spread across several pages. However, due to its density, it was hard to read, and it was literally changing under us as product management made changes for the impending announcements.

We debated and felt that the best thing we could do for our readers would be to provide a URL hyperlink, so that the most up to date information (and not stale or incorrect information!) is available to you. There are detriments to this approach, such as the dreaded 'busted URL', but in this day and age it's likely that you are reading this on a device with an Internet connection, or have one within reach, and as well we have the capability to update this book as soon as we find that something is amiss. You can find the features grid at:

http://www.slideshare.net/ibmdatapower/ibm-datapower-gateways-features-comparison

Acknowledgements

The Author Team:

We thank the IBM management team for allowing us to access the resources necessary to write the book.

The author team would like to thank Simon Kapadia for his contributions to the first edition and first version of this second edition volume, Colt Gustafson for his technical review, and the following people for technical contributions, clarifications, and suggestions for this book: Jaime Ryan (first edition co-author), Arif Siddiqui (including updates to the performance info), Bhargav Perepa, Chris Cross, Shiu-Fun Poon, Russell Butek, Trey Williamson, Colt Gustafson, David Maze, David Shute, Eugene Kuznetsov, Gari Singh, Greg Truty, Henry Chung, Joel Smith, John Graham, Julie Salamone, Ken Hygh, Keys Botzum, Rich Groot, Marcel Kinard, Rich Salz, Steve Hanson, Tom Alcott, Naipaul Ojar, Davin Holmes, Jon Harry, and Paul Glezen.

Bill Hines:

I'd like to thank Keys Botzum and Kyle Brown for being role models for work ethic and integrity, and mentoring me throughout my IBM career. I'd like to thank my immediate and extended family for being supportive and understanding during the tough times. Last, I'd like to thank my author team for sticking with this project during the many months, nights, and weekends of heated debates and stress. You were all picked for a reason, and I think the fact that you have all put up with me, and we have been through what we have and emerged still good friends with tremendous respect for each other, attests to those decisions being good ones. I'm extremely proud of the job you've done.

John Rasmussen:

I was lucky enough to have joined DataPower during its initial startup phase, and to have worked with some truly talented and inspirational people through its acquisition by IBM. The list is too long, but I'd like to thank Eugene Kuznetsov for making this all possible and for providing me with the opportunity to participate, Rich Salz for his generosity of time and knowledge and the many contributions he made to DataPower, Brian Del Vecchio for making building the WebGUI fun. And the many individuals who I came to respect and to rely on in tough times including; Jan-Christian Nelson, Gari Singh, David Maze, John Shriver, Tony Ffrench, James Ricotta, Shiu-Fun Poon and many others within and beyond the DataPower and IBM families. To my fellow authors, with a special word of appreciation to Bill Hines, as there is no doubt that without Bill's tremendous effort and continuous dedication these books would not have happened.

Jim Brennan:

I would like to thank all of my co-authors for including me in the writing of this book and for making it the best that it could be. I would especially like to thank Bill Hines for getting the band back together to get the latest information out there in this, and future volumes. I would like to thank my family and friends for being understanding and supportive when the stress seemed to be getting the best of me.

Ozair Sheikh:

I would like to thank my co-authors for giving me the opportunity to contribute to this book. A special thanks to Bill Hines whose hard work and leadership made this book a reality. I have been fortunate to work with a talented group of people during my career. Special thanks to my managers who recognized my contributions and provided me with opportunities to grow. I would also like to thank my IBM colleagues, Arif Siddiqui, Robert Conti, Ken Hygh, Tony Ffrench, Shiu-Fun Poon, Rachel Reinitz, Salman Moghul and Fred Tucci. I would like to thank my family and friends for supporting me in reaching my career goals.

About the Authors

Bill Hines

Bill is an IBM Executive I/T Specialist. His current role is as WebSphere Federal Chief Technical Architect and Strategist, working out of Lake Hopatcong, NJ. He has many years of IBM WebSphere solution design and implementation experience in both customer engagements and developing and delivering internal training within IBM. He is the lead author of the acclaimed book IBM DataPower Handbook (first and second editions) and co-author of IBM WebSphere: Deployment and Advanced Configuration, as well as many articles published in WebSphere Technical Journal and developerWorks. He is a United States Air Force veteran and has a Bachelor of Science degree from New York Institute of Technology and an Associate Degree in Information Technology from Tulsa Jr College.

John Rasmussen

John is a Senior Engineer within the IBM DataPower organization. John has been with IBM and DataPower since 2001 and has worked as a product development engineer (where he created and developed the original WebGUI Drag and Drop Policy Editor) and as a product specialist assisting many clients in the implementation of DataPower devices. John has an extensive career in software development, including work with McCormack & Dodge/D&B Software, Fidelity Investments and as an independent consultant. John has a degree from the University of Massachusetts at Amherst, and lives in Gloucester, Massachusetts.

Jim Brennan

Jim is a partner and president of an independent consulting firm, McIndi Solutions. McIndi Solutions is an IBM business partner based out of Hackettstown, NJ specializing in DataPower administration and configuration. Jim has assisted in developing and delivering internal DataPower education material to IBM consultants and engineers. Jim has also been an application developer working with several different programming languages and platforms ranging from COBOL to Java. Jim has been a JEE developer for several years specializing in JEE development for WebSphere Application Server. He also has several years of experience with WebSphere Application Server installation, configuration, troubleshooting, and administration. Jim has more than ten years of I/T experience with a certificate from the Chubb Institute of Technology and also attended Felician College in Lodi, NJ.

Ozair Sheikh

Ozair is a Senior Product Line Manager for IBM DataPower Gateways and certified IBM IT Specialist. He is an experienced SOA/ESB/Mobile IT professional with over 10 years in managing, consulting, instructing and developing enterprise solutions using WebSphere technologies. He is avid speaker at several worldwide conferences; topics ranging from Mobile security, API Management and architecting mission-critical ESB systems.

In his current role, Ozair helps drive new innovative solutions for the DataPower gateway platform that reflect customer requirements and market trends. Ozair holds a bachelor of Mathematics with specialization in Computer Science from the University of Waterloo. In his spare time, he is an avid hockey and basketball fan, and enjoys writing mobile apps to solve his everyday problems.

Afterword

Afterword by Eugene Kuznetsov

"The proper planning of any job is the first requirement. With limited knowledge of a trade, the job of planning is doubly hard, but there are certain steps that any person can take towards proper planning if he only will."

—Robert Oakes Jordan, Masonry

I founded a company called DataPower® in the spring of 1999 to build products based on several distinct ideas. The first idea involved applying reconfigurable computing and dynamic code generation to the problem of integrating disparate applications. The second idea centered on the concept of data-oriented programming (DOP) as the means to achieve direct and robust data interchange. The third idea involved delivering middleware as a network function, enabled by the DOP technology and inspired by the successful models of ubiquitous connectivity. The product's journey since has been remarkable, and this great book is another milestone for the entire team behind DataPower. Before more discussion of the book itself, a few words on these three ideas.

Rapidly adapting to change is key for everything and everyone in today's world, and IBM appliances are no exception. Whether it's a policy, a transformation map, a schema, or a security rule, DataPower will try to put it into effect with as little delay and interruption as possible. Popular methods for maintaining this kind of flexibility come with a large performance penalty. However, by dynamically generating code and reconfiguring hardware based on the current message flow, it became possible to achieve both flexibility and near-optimal performance. At any given point, the device operates as a custom engine for a particular task, but when the task changes, it can rapidly become a different custom engine underneath the covers.

This dynamic adaptability is especially useful when combined with DOP. Stated briefly, DOP emphasizes formally documenting data formats and using them directly, instead of encapsulation or abstraction, to integrate or secure different modules or systems. Today, XML is probably one of the most successful and readily recognized examples of DOP, but the principles are more universal than any particular technology. Another example of DOP is the way DataPower XI52 processes binary data, by using high-level format descriptors instead of adaptors.

These, in turn, enable the creation of network hardware (also known as appliance) products that operate on whole application messages (rather than network packets) to integrate, secure, or control applications. Greater simplicity, performance, security, and cost-effectiveness were envisioned—and are now proven—with the appliance approach. Beyond the appliance design discipline, the success of IP & Ethernet networking in achieving universal connectivity has much to teach about the best way to achieve radically simplified and near-universal application integration.

Reading this book will enable you to benefit from the previous three ideas in their concrete form: the award-winning IBM products they became. From basic setup to the most powerful advanced features, it covers DataPower appliances in a readable tone with a solid balance of theory and examples. For example, Chapter 6 does a great job in explaining the big-picture view of device operation, and Chapter 22 gives a detailed how-to on extending its capabilities. With some of the most experienced hands-on DataPower practitioners among its authors, it provides the kind of real-world advice that is essential to learning any craft.

When learning IBM DataPower, there is one thing that may be more helpful and rewarding than remembering every particular detail, and that is developing an internal "mental model" of how the devices are meant to operate and fit into the environment. Especially when troubleshooting or learning new features, this "mental model" can make device behavior intuitive. Reading the following pages with an eye toward not just the details but also this mental model will speed both productivity and enjoyment.

In conclusion, I would like to use this occasion to thank the entire team, past and present, who made and continues to make DataPower possible. Their work and the passion of DataPower users is an inspiring example of how great people and a powerful idea can change the world for the better.

—*Eugene Kuznetsov, Cambridge, MA Founder of DataPower Technology, Inc. served as President, Chairman, and CTO at various points in the company's history, and then served as director of Product Management and Marketing, SOA Appliances at IBM Corporation.*

DataPower's first office is on the right. Photo courtesy of Merryman Design.

Afterword by Jerry Cuomo

It all started when I was asked to co-host an IBM Academy Conference on "Accelerators and Off-Loading" in 2004. I was feeling a little out of my element, so I decided to take some of the focus off me and put it on others. I had been reading about some of the new XML-centered hardware devices and was intrigued. I have always been interested in system performance. With XML dominating our emerging workloads (e.g., Service Oriented Architecture), the impact of XML performance on system performance was becoming increasingly important. Hence, I thought it would be a good idea to invite a handful of these XML vendors to our conference.

At the conference, the DataPower presentation was quite different from the others. It wasn't about ASICs or transistors; it was about improving time to value and total cost of operation. The DataPower presentation focused on topics that were also near and dear to me, such as systems integration, configuration over programming, and the merits of built-for-purpose systems. In essence, Eugene Kuznetsov, the DataPower founder and presenter, was talking about the value of appliances. While very intriguing, I couldn't help but feel curious about whether the claims were accurate. So, after the conference I invited Eugene to come to our lab in Research Triangle Park in North Carolina to run some tests.

I have to admit now that in the back of my mind, I operated on the principle of "keeping your friends close and your enemies closer." Behind my intrigue was a feeling of wanting to understand their capabilities so that we could outperform vendors with WebSphere® Application Server. The tests went well; however, the DataPower team was somewhat reluctant to dwell on the raw XML performance capabilities of their appliance. Feeling a little suspicious, I had my team run some raw performance experiments. The results were off the charts. Why wasn't the DataPower team flaunting this capability? This is when I had my "ah-ha" moment. While performance measured in transactions per second is important and part of the value equation, the overall performance metrics found while assessing time to value and overall cost of operation and ownership are the most critical performance metrics to a business. This is where the DataPower appliances outperform. I read a paper, written by Jim Barton, CTO and co-founder of Tivo, called "Tivo-lution." The paper was inspiring as it confirmed the motivations and aspirations that I've had ever since I led IBM's acquisition of DataPower in 2005. In the paper, Barton describes the challenges of making complex systems usable and how "purpose-built" computer systems are one answer to the challenge:

"One of the greatest challenges of designing a computer system is in making sure the system itself is 'invisible' to the user. The system should simply be a conduit to the desired result. There are many examples of such purpose-built systems, ranging from modern automobiles to mobile phones."

The concept of purpose-built systems is deeply engrained in our DNA at IBM. The name of our company implies this concept: International Business Machines.

IBM has a long history of building purposed machines, such as the 1933 Type 285, an electric bookkeeping and accounting machine. I can imagine this machine being delivered to an accountant, plugging it in, immediately followed by number crunching. The accountant didn't have to worry about hard drive capacity, operating system levels, compatibility between middleware vendors, or application functionality. It just did the job. I can also imagine it followed the 80/20 rule. It probably didn't do 100% of what all accountants needed. But it probably did 80% of what all accountants needed very well. Users just dealt with the remaining 20%, or learned to live without it.

"Business Machines, Again" is my inspiration. Our customers respond positively to the re-emergence of this approach to engineering products. It's all about time-to-value and total cost of operation and ownership. Appliances such as our WebSphere DataPower are leading the way in delivering on these attributes.

At the extreme, purpose-built systems, such as a Tivo DVR and an XI52, are built from the ground up for their purposes. While they might use off-the-shelf parts, such as an embedded Linux® OS, it is important that all parts are "right sized" for the job. Right-sizing source code in a hardware appliance is more like firmware (with strong affinity to the underlying hardware) than it is software. As such, the Tivo-lution paper describes the need to own every line of source code to ensure the highest level of integration and quality:

"...by having control of each and every line of source code...

Tivo would have full control of product quality and development schedules. When the big bug hunt occurred, as it always does, we needed the ability to follow every lead, understand every path, and track every problem down to its source."

The Tivo team even modified the GNU C++ compiler to eliminate the use of exceptions (which generate a lot of code that is seldom used) in favor of rigid checking of return code usage in the firmware. DataPower similarly contains a custom XML compiler that generates standard executable code for its general-purpose CPUs, as well as custom code for the (XG4) XML coprocessor card.

A physical appliance has the unparalleled benefit of being hardened for security. Jim talks about this in his Tivo paper:

"Security must be fundamental to the design...We wanted to make it as difficult as possible, within the economics of the DVR platform, to corrupt the security of any particular DVR."

The DataPower team has taught me the meaning of "tamper-proof" appliances, or more precisely "tamper-evident." Like the 1982 Tylenol scare, we can't stop you from opening the box, but we can protect you, if someone does open it. In fact, the physical security characteristics of DataPower make it one of the only technologies some of our most stringent customers will put on their network Demilitarized Zone (DMZ). If a DataPower box is compromised and opened, it basically stops working. An encrypted flash drive makes any configuration data, including security keys, difficult to exploit. "DP is like the roach motel; private keys go in, but never come out" is the way we sometimes describe the tamper-proof qualities of DataPower.

But the truth is, DataPower is not a DVR. DataPower is a middleware appliance. Middleware is a tricky thing to make an appliance out of. Middleware is enabling technology and by its nature is not specific to any application or vendor. The Tivo appliance is a specific application (TV and guide) that makes it somewhat easier to constrain:

"Remember, it's television. Everybody knows how television works."

"Television never stops, even when you turn off the TV set. Televisions never crash."

Hence, the challenge (and the art) in building a middleware appliance involves providing the right amount of constraint, without rendering the appliance useless. For example, DataPower does not run Java™ code (which is the primary means of customizing much of the WebSphere portfolio); instead, it uses XML as the primary mode of behavior customization. So, at some level, DP is not programmed, but instead it is configured. Now, for those who have used XML (and its cousin XSLT), you know that it's more than configuration; however, it is a constraint over Java programming, which has unbounded levels of customizability. The combined team of IBM and DataPower have been bridging this gap (of special to general purpose) effectively. We have recently added features to DP to allow it to seamlessly connect to IBM mainframe software (IMS™ and DB2®) as well as capabilities to manage a collection of appliances as if they were one.

IBM has a healthy general-purpose software business. Our WebSphere, Java-based middleware is the poster child for general-purpose middleware (write once, run almost everywhere). However, there is a place for business machines that are purposed built and focus on providing the 80 part of the 80/20 rule. We are heading down this path in a Big Blue way.

This book represents an important milestone in the adoption of DataPower into the IBM family. The authors of this book represent some of IBM's most skilled practitioners of Service Oriented Architecture (SOA). This team is a customer facing team and has a great deal of experience in helping our customers quickly realize value from our products. They have also been among the most passionate within IBM of adopting the appliance approach to rapidly illustrating the value of SOA to our customers. The authors have unparalleled experience in using DataPower to solve some of our customers' most stringent systems integration problems. This book captures their experiences and best practices and is a valuable tool for deriving the most out of your WebSphere DataPower appliance.

—*Jerry Cuomo, IBM Fellow, WebSphere CTO*

Afterword by Kyle Brown

I can still remember the day in late 2005 when Jerry Cuomo first called me into his office to tell me about an acquisition (then pending) of a small Massachusetts company that manufactured hardware devices.

"Wait a minute. Hardware??!?"

That's the first incredulous thought that went through my mind. Jerry was the CTO of the WebSphere brand in IBM, which had become the industry-leading brand of middleware based on Java. Why were we looking at a company that made hardware? Echoing the immortal words of Dr. "Bones" McCoy from the classic Star Trek series, I then thought,

"I'm a software engineer, not a hardware engineer, dang it!"

But as I sat in his office, Jerry wove me a story (as he had for our executives) that soon had me convinced that this acquisition did, in fact, make sense for WebSphere as a brand and for IBM as a whole. Jerry had the vision of a whole new way of looking at SOA middleware—a vision that encompassed efficient, special-purpose appliances that could be used to build many of the parts of an SOA. Key to this vision was the acquisition of DataPower, which gave us not only a wealth of smart people with deep experience in Networking, XML, and SOA, but an entry into this field with the DataPower family of appliances—notably the Integration appliance.

Since that day, I've never regretted our decision to branch out the WebSphere brand well beyond its Java roots. The market response to the introduction of the DataPower appliances to the brand has been nothing short of phenomenal. Far from distracting us, the ability to provide our customers with an easy-to-use, easy-to-install, and remarkably efficient hardware-based option for their ESB and security needs has turned out to be an asset that created synergy with our other product lines and made the brand stronger as a whole. It's been an incredible journey, and as we begin to bring out new appliances in the DataPower line, we're only now beginning to see the fundamental shift in thinking that appliance-based approaches can give us.

On this journey, I've been accompanied by a fantastic group of people—some who came to us through the DataPower acquisition and some who were already part of the WebSphere family—who have helped our customers make use of these new technologies. Bill, John, and the rest of the author team are the true experts in this technology, and their expertise and experience show in this book.

This book provides a wealth of practical information for people who are either novices with the DataPower appliances, or who want to learn how to get the most from their appliances. It provides comprehensive coverage of all the topics that are necessary to master the DataPower appliance, from basic networking and security concepts, through advanced configuration of the Appliance's features. It provides copious, detailed examples of how the features of the appliances work, and provides debugging help and tips for helping you determine how to make those examples (and your own projects) work. But what's most helpful about this book is the way in which the team has given you not just an explanation of how you would use each feature, but also why the features are built the way they are. Understanding the thinking behind the approaches taken is an enormous help in fully mastering these appliances. The team provides that, and provides you with a wealth of hints, tips, and time-saving advice not just for using and configuring devices, but also for how to structure your work with the devices.

This book is something the DataPower community has needed for a long time, and I'm glad that the authors have now provided it to the community. So sit back, crack open the book, open up the admin console (unless you have yet to take the appliance out of the box—the book will help you there, too!) and begin. Your work with the appliances is about to get a whole lot easier, more comprehensible, and enjoyable as well.

—*Kyle Brown, Distinguished Engineer, IBM Software Services and Support*

Printed in Great Britain
by Amazon.co.uk, Ltd.,
Marston Gate.